National F ..... .

MW00782497

LAW
ENFORCEMENT

To
CONSERVE
and
PROTECT

Luke Lukas
Vermilion Community College

COPPERHOUSE PUBLISHING COMPANY
930 Tahoe Blvd. #602
Incline Village, Nevada 89451
(702) 833-3131 · Fax (702) 833-3133
e-mail info@copperhouse.com
http://www.copperhouse.com/copperhouse

Your Partner in Education
with
"QUALITY BOOKS AT FAIR PRICES"

National Park Service
LAW ENFORCEMENT
To Conserve and Protect

Copyright © 1999 by Copperhouse Publishing Company

Library of Congress Catalog Number 98-73437
ISBN 0-942728-93-9 Paper Text Edition

2 3 4 5 6 7 8 9 10

Printed in the United States of America.

ACKNOWLEDGMENTS

Many people helped make this book possible. I am grateful to those rangers of the National Park Service who offered their stories and concerns: Jim Webster, Arches N.P.; Bruce Edmonston, Craters of the Moon NM; Norm Dodge, Acadia N.P.; Roger Moder, Big Bend N.P.; Charlie Peterson and Deb Kantou, Bryce Canyon N.P.; Tony Schetysle, Canyonlands N.P.; Tom Habeeker, Denali N.P.; Roger Semler, Glacier N.P.; Randy Coffman, Sequoia Kings Canyon N.P.; Mark Marshall, Yellowstone N.P.; Steve Gough, Crater Lake N.P.; Bruce McKeeman, Voyageurs N.P.; Larry Clark, Glen Canyon NRA; Kelly Bush, North Cascades N.P.; Dale Antonich, Lake Mead NRA; Bob Whiteman, Great Smoky Mountains N.P.; Jay Liggett, Evergades N.P.; Karen Ardoin, Halakala N.P.; Jim Unruh and Andy Ernths, Great Basin N.P.; Jay Wells, Wrangell St. Elias N.P.; Larry Van Slyke, Zion N.P.; Stu Kroll, Isle Royale N.P.; Larry Carr, Whiskeytown NRA; Chris Cruz, Yosemite N.P.; Larry Hakel, Shenandoah N.P.; Bob Powell, Theodore Roosevelt N.P.; Dee Renee' Ericks, Olympic N.P.; and Chuck Sypher and Dan Kirchner, Grand Canyon N.P. If I misspelled any names, please forgive me. In some cases, interviews were done over the telephone. Thanks to everyone for your support.

Others who were extremely helpful were Darrell Cook, Gil Goodrich, and Mark Arsenault, all of Coulee Dam National Recreation Area. These three individuals offered their time and personal input, for which I am grateful.

This book was guided by my friends and professors at the University of Idaho: Dr. Edwin Krumpe, Dr. John Hunt and Dr. Eric Jensen.

Finally, credit must be given to my beautiful wife, Nora Lukas. She was the force behind this book, and her encouragement kept me motivated. Last, but certainly not least, my daughter Rebecca Lukas who transported manuscripts between states.

I wish all those students and instructors who utilize this book the best. I hope they find this field as fascinating as those individuals who contributed to this project.

Leo "Luke" Lukas

PREFACE

This text was designed to present the student of law enforcement with the theory and practice of law enforcement in the backcountry of the National Park System of the United States. The principles applied within this text can be applied to wilderness areas within the national forests and areas under the control of the Bureau of Land Management and the U.S. Fish and Wildlife Service.

The objectives of this text are to:

√ Enable a student to gain an understanding of the historical development of law enforcement in the National Park.

√ Obtain an understanding of the law enforcement issues that exist in park backcountry and how they are being solved.

√ Understand the procedures which are necessary in order to gain compliance from violators.

√ Gain an understanding of the complexities involved in maintaining a balance between visitor freedom and park preservation.

√ Learn and develop the skills needed in proactive backcountry law enforcement.

Various issues of concern are presented to the student, such as drug manufacturing, archaeological theft, off-road vehicle use, criminal violations, and violations by unknowing violators. The text also familiarizes the student with the basics of constitutional law, criminal law, natural resource law, and the United States Code of Federal Statutes and Regulations.

The text is designed to create an awareness of the unique situation a backcountry law enforcement ranger will face in the enforcement of their regulations. Hopefully this text will encourage the student of park backcountry law enforcement to pursue further study in this area.

TABLE OF CONTENTS

CHAPTER 5

ARREST AND DETENTION IN THE BACKCOUNTRY

CHAPTER 1

INTRODUCTION TO THE
NATIONAL PARK SERVICE

L aw enforcement is a park management tool, similar to resource management techniques, public relations, and interpretation. In order to adequately protect both the resource and the visitor, the manager or ranger must be aware of the rules, regulations, and laws that exist and must be enforced. The enforcement may range from the presence of an officer to the arrest of an individual, depending upon the situation.

In order to preserve the park areas for now and future generations, some visitor behavior must be controlled. Law enforcement is an essential tool used in the accomplishment of the National Park Service's mission. The primary and proactive goal of the National Park Service law enforcement program is the prevention of criminal activities through resource education, public safety efforts, and deterrence. This book is directed at the National Park Service, but the principles and solutions found herein can be applied to all park and wilderness situations.

Law enforcement in the national parks and backcountry areas is not a recent development stemming from today's problems, it has been an important tool since the inception of our first national park. Law enforcement is the means by which government seeks to insure compliance with, compels obedience to, or identifies and apprehends individuals who violate laws and regulations enacted for the protection of life, resources, property, public peace, and societal well-being.

THE HISTORY AND BACKGROUND
OF NATIONAL PARK SERVICE PHILOSOPHY

In 1916, Congress passed the Organic Act which authorized the formation of the National Park Service. The language of the act gave the fledgling Park Service an almost impossible mission. It instructed the National Park Service to, "Conserve the scenery and natural and historic objects and wildlife therein and to provide for the enjoyment of the same in such manner and by such means as will leave them unimpaired for future generations." (Organic Act of 1916)

This act mandates that the parks be conserved in order for people to use and enjoy the parks now and in the future. This has proven to be a difficult task. Since the passage of the act, conservation and use have been involved in every decision, large or small. The instruction to conserve the parks unimpaired, while at the same time providing needed facilities for public use, seems to be a contradicting goal (e.g., a road cannot be constructed in a park without damaging the park's scenery).

How much conservation is enough before it hinders use? How much use is enough before it affects conservation? These are the questions left unanswered by early administrators. The first director of the National Park Service, Stephen Mather, affected policy for many years. The parks were his only concern. The one way to promote them, and therefore conserve them, was to publicize them (Shankland). The solution, as it appeared to Mather, was to build facilities, roads, campgrounds, visitor centers, hotels, and other amenities, in order to attract visitors to the parks. In this endeavor, he was more than successful.

The most difficult early decision concerning the park system involved the complex question of how to transport people through the parks. The parks were opened to automobile traffic prior to the establishment of the National Park Service in 1916. Road construction probably causes more damage to the parks than any other kind of development. The road itself can divert water drainage, cause the introduction of exotic plant species, and disrupt the behavior of many species of wildlife. The most bitter battles in the parks were fought over road construction projects (Everhart). The reconstruction of the Tioga Road in Yosemite is a prime example.

Stephen Mather decided to buy the Tioga Road, which was privately owned. He raised the funds by soliciting from friends and organizations, including the Sierra Club. He obtained $15,500 and paid the other half out of his own pocket (Everhart). The reason for this purchase was to encourage travel to Yosemite. Mather believed that increased visitation was the only policy which could save the National Park System.

The Tioga Road was narrow, winding and steep. It was also crucial to Yosemite access, linking several entrances on the west side of the Sierra Nevada with the single entrance for visitors approaching from the east (Runte). In order to provide access, the road had to be reconstructed. The completed Tioga Road has provided park visitors with the opportunity to drive through the most beautiful sections of any national park. But this pleasure was bought with a price. You cannot restore the wilderness this road has destroyed!

The framers of national park legislation understood that conservation and use must be carefully balanced. They came to the conclusion that an attempt to spell out precisely how much is enough would not work. They defined the spirit in which the parks are to be managed and the ultimate purpose for which the parks are set aside. They ensured that with every decision which affected the parks, the process must begin anew, each proposal must be thoughtfully appraised in the light of experience, the changing nature of park use, and the possible effect of each action upon the resource.

Nature preservation in the National Park System began decades before the first park was set aside by Congress. The seeds of the preservation idea were sown by early conservationists. Individuals, such as George Catlin, Henry David Thoreau, and Frederick Law Olmstead, proposed that wild areas be set aside for future generations to understand and enjoy.

George Catlin traveled the western areas of America in the mid-1800s. He was an artist with a renown reputation. Catlin chronicled his journeys on canvas. In the spring of 1832, Catlin found himself at the headwaters of the Missouri river. It was during this time that he made an entry in his journal calling for the establishment of a "Nation's Park" to set aside forever the beauty of the American West. Catlin also entered in his journal that the Indians should be provided for in these national parks. Catlin writes:

> What a splendid contemplation too, when one (who has travelled these realms, and can duly appreciate them) imagines them as they might in the future be seen (by some great protecting policy of government) preserved in their pristine beauty and wildness, in a magnificent park...

Catlin was not the first person to declare that land should be preserved because of its wildness, but he was the first to suggest that land be preserved in large parks for all the people of the nation.

Thoreau believed that the preservation of the world was based in wildness. In his lecture, "Walking," for the Concord Lyceum, he called for the establishment of parks, or as he stated:

> At present, in this vicinity, the best part of the land is not private property; the landscape is not owned, and the walker enjoys comparative freedom. But possibly the day will come when it will be partitioned off into so-called pleasure-grounds, in which a few will take a narrow and exclusive pleasure only, when fences shall be multiplied, and mantraps and other engines invented to confine men to the public road, and walking over the surface of God's earth shall be construed to mean trespassing on some gentleman's ground. . .

He thought that if the government did not take a stand, all of the wild places which are so beneficial to man's spirit would be taken over by rich and powerful people. Thoreau believed that the natural world symbolized spiritual truth as well as natural law. Thoreau questioned the materialistic goals of America as early as 1858. He may have been the world's first environmentalist. Thoreau lived without the luxuries of his day, at Walden Pond, in a house he built for very little money. His attempt to influence the establishment of a land preservation system went unheeded until after his death. Like other great men, his genius was unrecognized until years later.

Actually, the idea of preserving parks and development of gardens is as old as ancient Babylon, Greece and Rome. The idea was carried to feudal England, when the nobility began setting aside tracts of land as forest and game reserves (Hampton). This custom was transported across the Atlantic to the "new world." The idea did not gain strength because of the myth that America's resources were inexhaustible. The myth would soon be dissipated after the turn of the twentieth century. Americans were beginning to realize that forests and their beauty were being exhausted. This is exemplified by a federal land grant for a park or pleasuring grounds for the people, given to the state of California from the government of the United States in 1864 (Runte). This grant would later be withdrawn, and the area would become Yosemite National Park.

THE FIRST NATIONAL PARK

Yellowstone National Park was established as the first national park in the world by the United States Congress. It was signed into law by President Grant on March 1, 1872. The area has been touted as fascinating by early explorers and trappers. It wasn't until the Folsom, Cook and Peterson expedition in 1869 that these wild accounts of bubbling water and hot mud were

believed by the general public. A second expedition was organized by Nathaniel Langford. This expedition departed for
Yellowstone on August 22, 1870. It made extensive discoveries of
hot springs, towering falls, and other curiosities of nature. (Hampton) After Langford's return, he gave lectures in Helena, Minne-
apolis, New York City, and Washington, D.C., describing this
remarkable mountain wilderness. These lectures promoted the
idea of establishing a policy for a national park system, which
began with Yellowstone.

The idea of making Yellowstone a national park has been
credited to many individuals. The real credit can be traced back to
the Washburn Expedition, which Langford helped organize. The
actual place of conception was a campsite on the confluence of the
Firehole River and the Gibbons River. Cornelius Hedges' diary,
published in 1904, called for the establishment of a national park
to protect the region of Yellowstone from despoliation by private
interests. (Hampton)

The new Yellowstone Park was a high mountainous plateau
practically inaccessible from all directions and far to the west of
most settlement and development, so when the bill came before
the Congress, it was passed with indifference. There were few
objections to its passage because the land was not considered to
contain any important natural resources. The passage of this bill
did not mean that the Congress or the public were becoming aware
of their wasteful ways. Congress had considered selling this area
to private concerns because they were not in the "show business"
(Hampton).

The lack of concern for this new park could be seen in the lack
of direction or policy demonstrated by Congress. Yellowstone
was being "picked to the bones" by curiosity seekers and poachers. Finally law enforcement was brought to the park. It was a long
painful process because Congress did not want to pass the necessary laws . One gamekeeper was approved by the Congress—that
individual was the first backcountry park ranger, Harry Yount.
However, one ranger could not control the poaching that was
occurring in this immense new park.

In addition, administrative structure provided for the park was haphazard. Congress placed the control of the park in the hands of the Secretary of the Interior. He was given the responsibility to ensure that the Park would be preserved and protected from despoliation, and he was enjoined to make and enforce all regulations necessary to carry out the Congressional mandate. The Congressional Act of 1872 failed to provide for specific laws for the government of the region; it neither specified nor provided for punishment or legal machinery for its enforcement. No appropriations were forthcoming for roads or for the protection of the park from vandalism (Hampton).

The first superintendent of the new park was Nathaniel Langford. He was ordered to protect and preserve the new national park. He was free to use any money appropriated by Congress to carry out his orders; however, no money came from Congress . Langford tried in vain to secure funding from Congress. He also realized that if no legislation was provided by Congress for the enforcement of regulations and punishment for offenses, the administration of the new Park would be impossible. He was correct!

Langford found his position as superintendent to be a nominal job. With no funds available for protection or improvement, and no code of laws by which to regulate, it was impossible to supervise the large tract of wilderness. He was powerless to prevent violations, and he never suggested the use of a paid police force, as he was unpaid too (Hampton). Langford never succeeded in preventing or reducing the acts of destruction then under way in the park. There was a noted disappearance of game from the park and increased vandalism within the park. Langford resigned in disgust over the lack of Congress's responsibility towards the park.

In 1877, a new President, Rutherford B. Hayes, took office and appointed a new Secretary of Interior, Carl Schurz. Schurz appointed Philetus W. Norris as Superintendent of Yellowstone National Park on April 18, 1877. During this period of time the Congress voted to appropriate funds for the fledgling Park. With

$10,000 in new funding, Norris hired an assistant superintendent and the nation's first park ranger, Harry Yount. Norris soon realized that one ranger could not protect such a vast area. He convinced the Secretary of Interior, Schurz, that more rangers should be hired. Soon there were ten rangers in Yellowstone. These rangers proved to be a disappointment because they were political appointees and had no experience dealing with poachers and vandals. The animals were still being slaughtered. Even Superintendent Norris was taking advantage of the abundance of game, securing an abundant supply of winter meat. This was not in compliance with the mandate set forth by Schurz. He favored the strictest protection of the park's wildlife population. Norris hoped to strengthen his position with the Secretary and forwarded the first set of regulations for the Park to Shurz in 1881. Shurz approved the rules on May 4, 1881. (Hampton) They persisted through the early days of civilian administration. They included:

1. Cutting of timber within the park was strictly prohibited, also removal of mineral deposits or natural curiosities without the superintendent's permission.

2. Fires should be kindled only when actually necessary and immediately extinguished when no longer required.

3. Hunting, trapping, and fishing, except to procure food for visitors or actual residents, were prohibited.

4. No person would be permitted to reside permanently within the park without permission from the Department of the Interior.

5. The sale of intoxicating liquors was prohibited.

6. Trespassers or violators of the foregoing rules would be summarily removed from the park by the superintendent and his employees, who were authorized to seize "prohibited articles" in case of resistance to their authority or repetition of any offense.

The enforcement of these regulations proved to be impossible. Congress recognized the shortcomings of a civilian ranger force, and on June 20, 1882, they appointed the protection of Yellowstone National Park to the Department of War. The United States Army would enforce the regulations in Yellowstone Park, but the administration of the park would still fall to the Department of the Interior.

THE U.S. CAVALRY

Military protection of Yellowstone National Park served to remove the administration of the park from the political arena. Under the command of conscientious military commanders, the rules and regulations governing the park were revised and enforced, threats to the very existence of the park were overcome and a new policy of preservation was implemented. A precedent was established for a National Park System, and punitive legislation was obtained from the Congress.

The military government of the park seemed rather harsh at times. Careless visitors were admonished for their transgressions. The park was patrolled by mounted soldiers, poachers were arrested and expelled, and points of interest within the park were protected against wanton vandalism. Through the actions of the military, policy, later to be adopted by the National Park Service, was developing in bits and pieces. The first military commander of Yellowstone, Captain Moses Harris stated, "This wonderland should for all time be kept as near as possible in its natural and primitive condition." Another element of policy was established when in reply to a letter regarding the sale of buffalo to the park, in order to replace these dwindling animals, Harris stated:

> It is not the policy of the government to endeavor to make this Park attractive, by making a collection of domesticated animals, but rather to preserve the reservation in its natural condition

and to protect the existing game animals so that
they may breed in security.

These measures helped to establish Park Service policy.
Harris realized that even his cavalry unit was not adequate to
protect such a large area as Yellowstone. This fact aided in the
establishment of additional policy, the augmentation of the park
force with additional troops every summer season. This augmentation is reflected in today's park operations, the Park Service
utilizes the assistance of a large force of seasonal rangers every
summer.

Other policy concerning commercialization of the park was
established during the military control of the park. Captain Boutelle,
another military Superintendent of Yellowstone, protested a lease
of some land within the park to establish an elevator near the falls.
He stated that, "If a policy of 'commercialization' would result,
then the original purpose of the park would be prostituted." Thus
the commercialization of our first national park was temporarily
halted. Several decades later Aldo Leopold would comment,
"Recreational development is a job, not of building roads into
lovely country but of building receptivity into the still unlovely
human mind." (Leopold) This corrective process fell to the early
rangers and the calvary as it does today to the National Park
Service's frontcountry and backcountry rangers.

MISSION 66

In 1956, Mission 66 was proposed. The program was designed to overcome the inroads of neglect and to restore the parks
to the people. It was a period of rapid facility development. This
program was to be accomplished within ten years (1966). After
the war, the park system was short of funding and the resurgence
of visitors was staggering the system. The parks were plagued
with inadequate maintenance, protection, and development. In
1940, there were 161 parks and monuments in the system, with

visitation close to 17 million people, the Park Service had a yearly budget of $33,577,000. After the war in 1955, they managed 181 areas, with over 55 million visitors, on a budget which was less than the previous 15 years ($32,525,000) (Wirth). Thus, Mission 66 was begun to alleviate this problem.

Director Conrad Wirth presented this proposal at the Public Services Conference at Great Smoky Mountains National Park on September 18, 1955. It was decided that pilot studies be initiated at various parks in the system. The selected parks constituted a good cross section of the service's administrative, preservation, protection, development, and visitor use problems. They were Yellowstone, Chaco Canyon National Monument, Shiloh National Military Park, Adams Mansion National Historic Site, Fort Laramie National Historic Site, and Everglades National Park. These pilot studies pointed out the importance of a master plan in the development stages of the program.

The next step was to fund a small project to demonstrate what the National Park Service was trying to accomplish. Congress was approached with this request. The president was also interested in this project, and he asked that it be presented to a full cabinet meeting. The preparation for the cabinet meeting took months. President Eisenower approved of the plan and included it in his State of the Union Address on January 5, 1956. Eisenhower said:

> During the past year, the areas of our national parks have been expanded and new wildlife refuges have been created. The visits of our people to the parks have increased much more rapidly than have the facilities to care for them. The administration will submit recommendations to provide more adequate facilities to keep abreast of the increasing interest of our people in the great outdoors.

The ten year budget submitted for the program was 786,545,600. The growth of the National Park System actually pushed the budget up to one billion dollars for the ten year period.

The appropriations made available for the National Park Service by Congress increased from $32,915,000 in 1955 to $68,020,000 in 1957. Finally, Congress realized that parks had to be funded after they were established.

The policy established by Mission 66 is as follows:

1. Preservation of park resources was a basic requirement underlying all park management.

2. Substantial and appropriate use of the National Park System is the best means by which its basic purpose is realized and is the best guarantee of perpetuating the system.

3. Adequate and appropriate developments are required for public use and appreciation of an area and for prevention of overuse. Visitor experiences which derive from the significant features of the parks, without impairing them determine the nature and scope of development.

4. An adequate information and interpretive service is essential to proper park experience. The principal purpose of such a program is to help the park visitor enjoy the area and to appreciate it and understand it, which leads directly to improved protection through visitor cooperation in caring for park resources.

5. Concession type services should be provided only in those areas where required for proper, appropriate park experience, and where these services cannot be furnished satisfactorily in neighboring communities. Exclusive franchises for concessioners' services within the park should be granted only where necessary to insure provision for dependable public service.

6. Large wilderness areas should be preserved undeveloped except for simple facilities required for access, backcountry use and protection, and in keeping with the wilderness atmosphere.

7. All persons desiring to enter a park area may do so; however it may be necessary to place a limit on the number of visitors who may enter certain prehistoric and historic ruins and structures because of limitations of space or because only a restricted number may safely pass over or through them at one time. Lodging, dining, and camping facilities cannot be guaranteed every visitor.

8. Operating and public use facilities of both government and concessioners which encroach upon important park features should be eliminated or relocated at sites of lesser importance, either within or outside the park.

9. Where airports are needed, they should be located outside of park boundaries; and use of aircraft within the park areas of the system should be restricted to investigations, protection, rescue, and supply services.

10. Camping is an appropriate and important park visitor use in many parks, and every effort should be made to provide adequate facilities for this use.

11. Picnic grounds should be provided in areas where picnicking is an important element in the visitor day-use pattern.

12. A nationwide plan for parks and recreation areas as envisioned in the park, Parkway and Recreational Area Study Act of 1936 should be completed as promptly as possible so that each level of government—local, state and federal—may bear its share of responsibility in the provision of recreation areas and service.

13. Adequate and modern living quarters for National Park Service employees should be provided when

required for effective protection and management. Living quarters for government and concessioner employees, when located within the park, should be concentrated in a planned residential community out of public view.

14. The use of a park for organized events, organized sports, or spectator events which attract abnormal concentrations of visitors and which require facilities, services, and manpower above those needed for normal operations should not be permitted except in the National Capitol Parks (Wirth)

The guidelines set forth in this policy are still in use within the Park Service. Mission 66 was successful in meeting its objectives. Perhaps it was too successful; it established a mindset in the Park Service which emphasized development. The construction accomplishments of Mission 66 were many: 1,570 miles of park roads were reconstructed and 1,197 miles of new roads were built. Road construction is the most damaging activity to an environment. Five hundred miles of new trails were constructed and 330 new parking lots, 575 new campgrounds, 742 new picnic areas, 82 amphitheaters, 521 new water systems and 271 power systems, and 221 new administrative buildings were built. Other facilities and reconstructions of historic buildings and construction of employee residences were also completed under the policy of Mission 66.

Today, the actions and accomplishments of Mission 66 are being criticized by many environmental groups.

THE LAW ENFORCEMENT RANGER

The functions of a ranger have changed over the years. In the early days of the Park Service, the ranger was truly a man of all seasons. A ranger was a firefighter, a naturalist, a manager, an interpreter, a trail blazer, a game warden, a trail builder, and a biologist. But as they say, "Times are a changin." With modern day problems, come modern day solutions. The ranger, too, has become a specialist. The Park Service is now split into many divisions, and the trend is toward even more specialization. Some resource managers and interpretive rangers hold law enforcement commissions. In order to describe the functions of a ranger, one must now ask, what division does he or she belong to?

The ranger division is divided into three sections:

1) Law enforcement

2) Resource management

3) Interpretation

The major impetus for adding law enforcement to the rangers' bag of tools was an event that the National Park Service called the Stoneman Meadow Riots. The incident began in the afternoon on July 4, 1970, when a group of disgruntled would-be campers set up their tents in Stoneman Meadows in the middle of Yosemite Valley, after learning that the park campgrounds were filled. Rangers ordered the campers to move, and the squatters responded by throwing rocks and bottles at the rangers. The National Park Service was totally unprepared for the violent encounter. By the time the uprising was quelled, much of the conventional understanding of what rangers should be doing was irreversibly altered. The National Park Service conducted an investigation of the riots and how they were handled. The recommendations that followed called for field rangers to be trained in law enforcement. Another recommendation was that park police be brought into the parks. However, National Park Service management was concerned that the public would be adversely affected if law enforcement was too conspicuous and decided to give park rangers sole responsibility for crime control. In 1976, Congress passed the General Authorities Act, making law enforcement a requirement for park rangers who patrol parks as part of their regular duties.

In those first days of law enforcement, rangers were handed badges and guns and learned to use them on the job. Today, park rangers must earn their law enforcement commissions; the National Park Service requires that permanent rangers attend the Federal Law Enforcement Training Center (FLETC) in Glyncoe, Georgia. Seasonal law enforcement rangers must attend a seasonal academy and receive approximately 300 hours of law enforcement training. The basic course at FLETC now takes approximately 11 weeks and includes courses about firearm handling, arrest techniques, communication skills, legal training, and crime scene investigation. To supplement their skills, commissioned permanent rangers can take special courses in wildlife law, archaeological resource protection, search and rescue and many others. In addition to all of this training, the Department of the Interior requires that both permanent and seasonal rangers attend a 40 hour refresher course each year.

THE EMERGING ROLE OF LAW ENFORCEMENT

In recent years, rising crime in the national parks has resulted in the transformation of the role of the ranger from that of a naturalist and interpreter to that of a police officer. Even rangers in the park backcountry and wilderness must make arrests, issue citations, and investigate crimes.

During "Operation Trophy Kill," Yellowstone rangers worked with U.S. marshals and local sheriffs in both intelligence and as arresting officers. This 1984 sting operation broke an international poaching ring that had been preying on park elk, grizzly, and bighorn sheep. They sold antlers, paws, horns and other animal parts nationally and internationally. In 1985, at Richmond National Battlefield Park in Virginia, rangers and county deputies conducted a night stakeout to catch thieves who were robbing the park's civil war graves for artifacts. The arrests resulted in the first convictions under the Archaeological Resource Protection Act.

— Real Life Situation ———————————

On June 19, 1993, several young people camping in Brooklyn Bottom at New River Gorge in West Virginia passed through an adjacent camp occupied by two couples over a period of about an hour while enroute to the New River to fish. One of them entered the camp just to talk and be social. During the conversation, one of the individuals in the camp told the other person to leave and that he wanted the entire group to pack up and leave the area. He became increasingly belligerent. There were some verbal confrontations with other members of the 12 person group during which the man involved made threats and ordered them out of the area. The man then took up a shotgun, brandished it, made more threats, and fired it in the direction of the group of 12. No one was hit by the blast, and there were no injuries during the confrontation. The group immediately packed up and left the area. After receiving a report of the incident, rangers responded and investigated. The man was charged with assault with a deadly weapon, brandishing a firearm, and possession and use of a firearm.

During the first two weeks of June 1993, rangers in the Everglades National Park participated in an interagency task force to counter illegal dumping activities occurring in designated wetlands in and around the park. The task force included rangers, FBI agents, the Metro–Dade Police Department, and Metro–Dade Environmental Resources Department. Four arrests were made, including one individual who was illegally operating his own Hurricane Andrew debris removal service. The operation was closely coordinated with the U.S. attorney's office, which plans to file felony charges against those arrested for filling wetlands without a permit. The operation involved 20 officers and a spotter aircraft.

Gangs of youth roam the backcountry at Lake Mead National Recreation area. Methamphetamine manufacturers have invaded Death Valley National Monument. The poachers are still at work in the Great Smoky Mountains National Park, Rocky Mountain National Park, Yellowstone National Park and many others. The war to protect our backcountry is still on.

All areas of the system are experiencing more crime. More arrests are made in Yosemite National Park than in any other park in the National Park System. Yosemite has a full-time jail with a holding capacity of 16; it is often overfilled. Between 800 and 900 arrests are made in Yosemite annually, not including citations for minor offenses. To contrast this statistic, consider that in 1950 only 15 people were arrested in Yosemite for the entire year. Today, Yosemite rangers arrest 50 people a night during the busy summer season.

The National Park Service believes the rise in park crime parallels the growth in recent years of the number of visitors, especially in heavily trafficked parks near urban areas. In 1940, there were 161 parks and monuments in the system, with visitation close to 17 million people, the Park Service had a yearly budget of $33,577,000. After the war in 1955, they managed 181 areas, with over 55 million visitors, on a budget which was less than the previous 15 years, $32,525,000 (Wirth). In 1960, approximately 10.7 million people visited the major nature parks in the National Park System. By 1982 the number had risen to 344.4 million and offenses in the parks stood at 87,153. In 1987, the NPS recorded 364.6 million visits with 127,322 offenses.

The problem is not just with numbers of visitors, it is also related to the type of visitor. In recent years, the traditional family campers and solitude seeking wilderness backpackers have been joined by visitors whose idea of having fun does not coincide with park protection.

The author's research has shown that the greatest increase in crime is in drug and alcohol-related crimes, vandalism, natural resource violations and off-road vehicle violations. In park frontcountry areas, traffic violations have increased the most.

The safety of park visitors is a concern for the National Park Service. In some of our parks, visitors are not safe when they are alone. The parks are becoming places where violence, pollution, overpopulation, and corruption are commonplace. The ranger is no longer a naturalist and interpreter but a policeman. The ranger is trained in defensive tactics, constitutional law, arrest techniques, and firearms use. The parks are not even safe for rangers. In 1988, there were 86 assaults on National Park Service rangers. (Frome)

Law enforcement has changed the ranger image. In addition, there has been a shift in the personality of rangers, which may be directly attributed to their additional law enforcement duties. Rangers, like their police counterparts, are confronted with the "us vs. them" mentality. When rangers deal with people who lie to them when caught because they fear going to jail; people who have committed a crime; and people under the influence of drugs and alcohol; the ranger begins to perceive another side of the park visitor—the seamy side. This may be leading to the formation of a police subculture within the National Park Service. This trend must be counteracted if the Park Service is to perpetuate its original mission. The ranger must still interact with the visitor. The traditional image of a friendly park ranger must be kept intact. The purpose of this book is to teach how to enforce the law but still retain the traditional ranger image.

In order to preserve this traditional ranger image, a philosophy of low key law enforcement must be implemented. This means that rangers must use the lowest level of law enforcement that will prevent the reoccurrence of a violation; however, this does not mean that no action should be taken. The philosophy of low key law enforcement and the ethical behavior which must accompany it will be further explained and discussed in Chapter 5. Without knowledge of ethics and the desire to live by them, a ranger would not be a ranger.

In addition to understanding and practicing law enforcement ethics, all backcountry rangers must have a good basis in constitutional law, criminal law (both federal and state) and a working knowledge concerning the regulations which they will enforce in the park. A brief synopsis is presented in Chapter 2. It is strongly suggested that every person who is seriously considering a career in backcountry law enforcement take as many courses as possible in these subjects. The knowledge of the law will be reflected in how the ranger does his/her job. How the ranger conducts his/herself affects his/her image.

What is it that really affects the visitor's image of a ranger? Are visitors affected by the defensive equipment a ranger wears, or the fact that the ranger must enforce regulations aimed at petty infractions, such as dogs off leash, illegal camping and campfires and off-road driving? The enforcement of regulations which control the behavior of visitors and the equipment used by rangers will be discussed in future chapters. The visitor normally doesn't mind if rangers investigate crime and arrest felons, but they object to being stopped for the minor infractions many visitors commit.

Ranger activity or "rangering" includes recovering and returning stolen property of a visitor; keeping the campgrounds quiet in order that the visitor will have a pleasant experience; resource protection that results in a clean pristine area for visitors to enjoy; removing drunk drivers and enforcing traffic laws on park roads; controlling unknowing violators in the parks; and deciding what to do with a violator who is far from the nearest road or other rangers.

There is nothing negative about the direct enforcement of laws and regulations. They are important for a safe, enjoyable visitor experience in the parks. The negative aspect comes into play when rangering is performed in a negative manner by a ranger with a negative attitude. We all must strive to eliminate the negative attitude initiated by the "us against them" mentality.

In summary, the National Park Service has utilized a low key law enforcement philosophy since its inception. The parks have been, and still are, subject to overuse and degradation. It is the job of the NPS law enforcement ranger to preserve and protect the lands of the National Park Service for the enjoyment of future generations. This text is designed with this goal in mind.

References

Everhart, William C., *The National Park Service* (New York: Praeger Publishers) 1972.

Foresta, Ronald A., *America's National Parks and Their Keepers* (Washington D.C.: Resources for the Future) 1984.

Frome, Michael, *Regreening The National Parks* (Tuscon: University of Arizona Press) 1992.

Hampton, Duane H., *How The U.S. Cavalry Saved Our National Parks* (Bloomington: Indiana University Press) 1971.

Leopold, Aldo, *A Sand County Almanac* (New York: Oxford University Press) 1949.

Runte, Alfred, *National Parks, The American Experience* (Lincoln: University of Nebraska Press) 1979.

Shankland, Robert, *Steve Mather of the National Parks* (New York: Alfred A. Knopf) 1970.

Wirth, Conrad L., *Parks, Politics, and People* (Norman: University of Oklahoma Press) 1980.

Chapter 2

Laws and
the National Park Service

Т he Constitution, in concert with its various amendments, forms the framework of our criminal justice system. It specifies how we will protect society from criminal threats while insuring that personal freedoms and liberties are preserved. This chapter is a study of the laws, regulations, and guidelines under which backcountry law enforcement rangers operate in properly exercising their authority.

The sworn peace officer takes an oath to uphold the Constitution and the law of his or her jurisdiction. The National Park Service challenges its sworn rangers to achieve high standards of job performance. How often does an officer arrest an innocent person? The answer is—always. Remember that everyone is innocent until they are proven guilty in a court of law. The Constitution of the United States was established to ensure that all of our citizens would be treated fairly and equally under our laws. It is the responsibility of all law enforcement officers to uphold the Constitution.

DM446—The Departmental Manual

The DM446, Interior's Departmental Manual, was established with a specific purpose—the resources must be protected. The overall goal of law enforcement within the National Park Service is to prevent harmful or unlawful acts. Public Law 94-458 states that the Secretary of Interior can designate certain employees of the Department of Interior to enforce its regulations. The

DM446 is the Department of Interior's law enforcement manual and includes standards which require an officer to possess intelligence, tact, sound judgement, emotional stability, and a good personality. The NPS law enforcement ranger, both seasonal and permanent, must comply with the standards set forth by the Department of Interior's DM446.

The National Park Service Guidelines (NPS 9) and DM446 state how the ranger is to conduct law enforcement. The ranger will be identified as a law enforcement officer, assigned as a law enforcement officer, and commissioned as a law enforcement officer. All rangers will be required to attend law enforcement training as designated by the current NPS-9. All law enforcement rangers in uniform will carry defensive equipment, which includes a firearm. The goal of law enforcement is the safety of the park visitor, protection of the resources, enhancement of the visitors enjoyment, and protection of the property of the park.

NATIONAL PARK SERVICE LAW ENFORCEMENT

"The spirit of the law is more important than the letter of the law." This means the National Park Service strives to accomplish its goals using the lowest level of law enforcement possible. Courtesy to the visitor is considered to be an important aspect of the law enforcement ranger's position. Citations should not be written until the visitor is made aware of the rules and regulations governing the national parks. These are the 36 Code of Federal Regulations (CFR's). If a verbal warning will not suffice, a written warning is the next step. If the visitor continues to violate the regulations, the ranger is left with no choice but to issue a citation or to make an arrest. The most common and serious violations will be discussed in future chapters.

In many parks, the extent of verbal and written warnings is determined by park management. Some violations may not be posted, yet the average visitor to an area is well aware of the violation, and a citation may be the most appropriate method of handling the situation. For example, at the Coulee Dam National Recreation Area, beach fires are prohibited. The average visitor to the area has visited the park three previous times; therefore, park management deems it appropriate to issue a citation for illegal beach fires upon the first encounter. Elsewhere this also applies to campfires above the tree level in parks like Rocky Mountain and Olympic. Education must be emphasized as the primary mode of law enforcement. Always give the violator a resource message. Explain to the person why the thing he/she did was wrong. Our purpose is not to punish behavior but to correct behavior. The visitor should leave the park with a good impression of the service, the park, and the ranger.

━━ Real Life Situation ━━━━━━━━━━━━━━

A ranger working on the Coulee Dam National Recreation Area in east central Washington approached a violator who was maintaining an illegal beach campfire. The ranger explained why fires were not allowed on the beaches of Lake Roosevelt. He said that there was a serious fire danger because of fires which are left unattended, and he spoke about the impacts they cause to the resource. The ranger's attitude was extremely positive, but in spite of a positive attitude, he was met with animosity from the violator. The person screamed at the ranger and accused the ranger of imposing restrictive regulations upon the general public. The person's tone became increasingly threatening. The ranger decided that a warning and a resource message would not work to gain compliance in this situation. The ranger told the individual that he was going to receive a citation for this violation. The news was greeted with another blast of profanity and an increase in hostility. The person then tried to assault the ranger. The assault was thwarted. There are times when the low key approach will not work to gain compliance, but it should always be the initial approach if possible.

The first thing which should be in the mind of the ranger is the safety of the visitors and employees of the National Park Service and its concessionaires. There are certain steps which can be taken to ensure the safety of the visitor. These range from the mere presence of the ranger to the use of deadly force. This continuum will be discussed in a later chapter on the use of physical force.

The jurisdiction of National Park Service rangers is basically territorial. *Jurisdiction* is where an officer can take law enforcement actions. *Authority* is when or how an officer can take law enforcement action within his/her specific park.

Jurisdiction is a method of limiting a territory in which authority may be exercised. The only exceptions to a ranger's jurisdiction is when an officer is in hot pursuit or when serving warrants outside of the park. There are four categories of jurisdiction among land management law enforcement agencies: exclusive, concurrent, partial, and proprietary jurisdiction.

1. Exclusive jurisdiction. This is a special type of authority to enforce federal laws within a park. In other words, "The Federal Government has received all the authority of the state, with no reservations made to the state except the right to serve process papers resulting from activities which occurred off the land involved." (FLETC, 1992 p. USC3)

— Situation —————————————

A vehicle is stopped by a ranger in Yellowstone for not having both headlamps operational. There is no federal law which is applicable in this scenario. The ranger would assimilate state law by using 36 CFR 4.2 (b). In this type of jurisdiction, a state officer would not be able to enter the park and enforce the same state law.

In this type of jurisdiction, state law can be assimilated into federal law and enforced by way of federal statute; therefore, state law becomes federal law. Yellowstone National Park is an exclusive jurisdiction park. The park was established prior to the state of Wyoming; therefore, federal law is the only law to be enforced in Yellowstone National Park. This has caused a lot of controversy throughout the bordering states of Montana, Wyoming and Idaho.

2. Concurrent jurisdiction. This type of jurisdiction is similar to exclusive jurisdiction except that federal and state law both apply to the park. It is defined as follows: "Where the state has granted authority which would otherwise amount to exclusive jurisdiction over an area but the state has reserved to itself the right to exercise concurrently with the United States, all state authority." (FLETC, 1992 p. USC3)

    The state laws can be enforced within the park by federal officers and by state officers. The state law is assimilated under a special regulation in the 36 CFRs. Federal law is exclusively administered by federal officers within a concurrent jurisdiction park. At certain times, it benefits the ranger to assimilate state law instead of using federal law. One of those instances concerns violations which involve juveniles. There is no provision made for juveniles in the federal law.

    If a state or county officer observed a violation in a park with concurrent jurisdiction, he/she would be able to enter the park lands and enforce state law only. In a concurrent jurisdiction, state officers are able to enforce the law in the park as well as the rangers.

— Real Life Situation —————————

A county deputy was making a regular patrol through an area of a park at the request of a ranger who would not be on duty late at night. The county officer located a party in which the participants were all underage individuals. The

officer cited and released all of the juveniles to
their parents. The benefit of concurrent jurisdiction provided this additional coverage to the
park under this type of jurisdiction.

3. Partial jurisdiction. Partial jurisdiction is when the
    state gives the federal government that which is ap-
    proved by the state legislature. In other words, "The
    Federal Government has been granted the right to
    exercise certain of the state's authority, with the state
    reserving the right to exercise by itself, or concur-
    rently with other authority beyond the mere right to
    serve process papers (e.g., the right to tax private
    property)" (FLETC, 1992 p. USC4). This means that
    you can enforce all federal rules and regulations in the
    park, but you cannot enforce state laws upon those
    lands, unless the state has given prior approval of the
    enforcement of a particular state statute. Only state
    officers can enforce state law within those jurisdic-
    tions. This does not apply to special maritime jurisdic-
    tion laws.

4. Proprietary interest jurisdiction. This only applies to
    the federal government as a land owner. FLETC
    (1992, pg USC4) defines this as, "The Federal Gov-
    ernment has acquired some right or title to an area in
    a state but has not obtained any measure of the state's
    authority over the area." This gives the park authority
    to enforce such state laws as no trespassing laws. This
    type of jurisdiction does not give the park rangers the
    authority to enforce any other state laws except those
    that would apply to any other land owner; however, it
    does allow the park to enforce all federal laws within
    the jurisdiction of that particular park.

— **Situation** ————————————————

Most Utah national parks only have proprietary jurisdiction. In these jurisdictions, state
traffic laws and other such laws can only be
enforced by state or local officers. If an individual violates a state law within the park, such
as a law which prohibits domestic abuse, a state
officer will be called to finalize the arrest. This
does not mean that the ranger must stand idly
by and watch. The ranger can, and will, stop the
individuals and detain them, but he will not take
them into custody until the state authorities
arrive. The ranger may transport the individuals to a state facility and turn them over there.

All rangers should find out what type of jurisdiction applies
to their prospective park before they start work.

NPS-9

NPS-9 guidelines are utilized by the National Park Service in
order to guide law enforcement operations throughout the United
States. I will give a brief overview of the NPS-9 in the following
pages. They are administered uniformly throughout the National
Park System. Deviation from these guidelines is allowed only in
those cases where a section allows a supplemental policy by an
individual park or region. The guidelines address law enforcement principles, such as objectivity, adaptability, integrity, versa-
tility, and compatibility. It also sets forth the *National Park
Service Law Enforcement Code of Ethics*, which will be explained
in Chapter 7.

NPS-9 includes a chapter which governs the administration
of the law enforcement program. This includes the provision for

background investigations of potential officers and the issuance of law enforcement commissions. Another section of the guidelines covers the numerous training standards set forth by the National Park Service for its law enforcement rangers. Requirements range from first aid certification, firearms proficiency, criminal investigation training, emergency vehicle operations, and defensive equipment policy.

This extensive set of guidelines also establishes procedure for the convening boards of review which investigate accidents and shootings and deal with the post trauma such incidents may cause rangers who are involved in these situations. It addresses undercover operations, evidence management, and handling controlled substances. Finally, it stipulates how all incidents, both criminal and noncriminal, are to be reported and communicated through the various media and public relation outlets.

NPS-9 tries to be all encompassing, but what needs to be remembered is that it is a set of guidelines. It is being rewritten and updated year to year, and it is not meant to be the last word in law enforcement for the National Park Service. What it does set forth are general guidelines for enforcing the rules and regulations within our National Park System, as well as for the enforcement of laws set forth by the Congress of the United States.

CONSTITUTIONAL LAW

The Constitution of the United States governs what can and cannot be enacted into law by the U.S. Congress. Article IV, section 3, clause 2 (Property Clause) states:

> The Congress shall have Power to dispose of and make all needful rules and regulations respecting the Territory or the Property belonging to the United States; and nothing in this Constitution shall be so construed as to prejudice any claims of the United States, or of any particular state.

The national parks certainly fit under this Article. The rules and regulations which regulate the National Park System and

National Forests are written by the agencies in charge of their respective territory.

The Constitution has granted all power necessary to the Congress in order to properly run the government of the United States and the territory under its control. Again this includes the parks and forests and rangelands of our nation. Article I, section 8, clause 18, sets this out explicitly: The Congress shall have power ". . .to make all laws which shall be necessary and proper for carrying into execution the foregoing powers, and all other powers vested by this Constitution in the government of the United States, or in and Department of Officer thereof." This Article was tested by the states, and the U.S. Supreme Court ruled that Congress possesses the right to make all laws necessary in the case of *McCulloch v. Maryland* (17 US (4 Wheat) 316 1819).

Congress has enacted many laws which affect the natural resources of this country and its National Park System. Some of the more important laws and executive orders are:

- Antiquities Act of 1906 (16USC 433)
- Bald Eagle Act (16USC 668)
- Lacey Act (16USC 667e)
- National Environmental Policy Act (42 USC 4321, 4331-4335, 4341-4347, PL 91-190)
- Endangered Species Act (16USC 668, PL93-205))
- The Wilderness Act of 1964 (78 Statt. 890; 16 U.S.C. 1131-1136, PL 88-577)
- NPS Organic Act of 1916 (16USC 1, 2, to4, 22, 43)
- The General Authorities Act of 1976 (16USC 1a-6)
- The Free Roaming Wild Horse and Burro Act (16 U.S.C. 1331-1338, 1338a, 1339, 1340)
- Off Road Vehicle Regulations (EO 11644)
- The Archaeological Protection Act of 1979 (16USC 470)
- Act to Regulate Mining (PL94-429)

All of the preceding laws were enacted by the Congress of the United States under the auspices of the Constitution of the United States in order to protect the areas under its charge from violations, such as poaching, artifact collecting, plant collecting, degradation of historic features, degradation of natural features, livestock trespass, prospecting and mine claim location, timber cutting, dumping waste or hazardous materials, feeding wildlife, removing or diverting water, and preventing arson.

The rangers of the National Park Service are under oath to uphold the Constitution of the United States and the laws enacted by the Congress. The Constitution provides many safeguards against the police abuse of the citizens of this nation. The rights and cases affected by the Fourth, Fifth, Sixth, and Eight Amendments are numerous and consuming. Only a small segment of those rights, and the manner of protecting those rights, will be dealt with in this book. I recommend that extensive study be engaged in these subjects for those of you contemplating a career in backcountry law enforcement.

THE FOURTH AMENDMENT

One of the most difficult subjects for any law enforcement officer is the subject of search and seizure. There are numerous statutes and rules which cover the most minute portions of when a law enforcement officer can search and seize evidence or persons. Problems for officers arise when they must make spur of the moment decisions of whether to arrest or to seize or search for evidence. Substantial changes occur on a regular basis, new court decisions on what is a legal search, seizure, or arrest are forthcoming monthly. It may seem extremely confusing, but there are a few general guidelines which can make it a little less complicated. If followed, these guidelines can aid in ensuring that an officer's actions will be lawful and the evidence seized will be admissible in court. Let us begin with a brief discussion of the Fourth Amendment.

The Fourth Amendment states:

> The right of the people to be secure in their
> persons, houses, papers, and effects, against un-
> reasonable searches and seizures, shall not be
> violated, and no warrants shall issue, but upon
> probable cause, supported by oath or affirmation,
> and particularly describing the place to be searched,
> and the persons or things to be seized.

It is stated that warrants shall be based upon probable cause, but some searches only require reasonable suspicion and do not require probable cause or warrants. They must just be reasonable and lawful. Some examples would be consent searches and border searches. On the other hand, if a warrant is issued, it must be based upon articulated probable cause backed by oath or affirmation. The courts have allowed for warrantless searches based upon exigent circumstances. These circumstances must fall into a few specially established and well-delineated exceptions to the warrant requirements. When in doubt all law enforcement officers should make every effort to obtain a warrant.

Just what is *probable cause*? "Probable cause exists where the facts and circumstances within the officer's knowledge of which they had reasonable, trustworthy information, are sufficient in themselves to warrant a man of reasonable caution in the belief that an offense has been or is being committed." (*Brinegar v. United States*, 338 U.S. 160, 1949) A more concise definition would not serve an officer's purposes. It could never take into consideration the changing conditions all law enforcement officers find in their daily duties.

The most important point is that probable cause must consist of more than suspicion. There must be enough facts for a reasonable man to be satisfied that a crime has been committed. Remember that the very definition of probable cause implies probability. These are everyday factual and practical circumstances on which reasonable people act.

An arrest or seizure is valid if probable cause exists at the time of arrest or seizure. For example, an officer responds to the scene of a visitor confrontation where he observes two individuals covered with bruises and dirt. The individuals are still faced off, prepared to do battle again, and there are a dozen witnesses. There is sufficient probable cause for a reasonable prudent person to believe that the individuals are guilty of the crime of disorderly conduct. On the other hand, if a ranger by chance encounters two individuals covered with dirt and a couple of bruises, the individuals could have been engaged in any number of activities, there is not enough probable cause to establish that a crime had been committed.

Another important point that must be kept in mind is that probable cause does not establish guilt. It is not up to the individual officer to determine guilt or innocence, only to effect an arrest if probable cause exists. There is no magic rule or guideline in the determination of probable cause. Each situation must be decided on its own facts and circumstances. An officer must also rely upon his/her own training and experience in determining if probable cause exists in order to effect an arrest.

The ideal method of making an arrest is to obtain an arrest warrant from a judge or magistrate based upon probable cause. This is often impractical or impossible depending upon the situation. It is a common practice to arrest without a warrant. When doing so, a few simple rules must be remembered in addition to the probable cause requirement. Felony arrests are legal if they are based upon reasonable grounds, and misdemeanor arrests are allowed if the offense occurs in the ranger's presence. When an officer is arresting individuals, he should make sure enough facts are available to have enabled him to obtain a warrant if the time were available.

THE EXCLUSIONARY RULE

Prior to 1914, all evidence obtained was not affected by the illegality or legality of how it was obtained. The Court would make no inquiry as to how it was obtained. As long as it was relevant and competent, evidence it was admissible.

In 1914, the U.S. Supreme Court ruled that if evidence was illegally obtained by federal officers it was not admissible in court. This new ruling became known as the Exclusionary Rule.

The purpose of this rule was to prevent officers from violating the Constitutional rights of the citizens of the United States by removing the incentive to do so (NPS, 1984). This rule simply means that an officer may not use the results of an illegal search.

The Exclusionary Rule does not apply to evidence seized under a warrant where officers acted in good faith, even though the warrant may not be valid due to other circumstances, such as inadequate probable cause or an improper signature. This exception does not apply if the magistrate or judge was misled by the officer or if the magistrate totally disregarded his mandate to remain neutral.

Volumes upon volumes of texts have been written explaining the nuances of the Fourth Amendment. . .when to administer the *Miranda* warning, what the Plain View Doctrine covers, when is a search legal without a warrant... all of these subjects must be thoroughly understood by law enforcement officers, whether they enforce the law in the backcountry of our national parks and wilderness or on the streets of our largest cities. The International Association of Police has set forth a few simple guidelines which cover the restrictions of searching (1966). "First, searches may only be made for certain classes of materials, specifically:

1. The tools of the crime
2. The fruits of the crime
3. Contraband
4. Goods on which an excise tax is due

Secondly, the American courts have held that searches may be carried out:

1. With a search warrant that conforms to the requirements of the Fourth Amendment
2. As incidental to an arrest
3. Without a search warrant but with consent of the person to be searched or the proprietor of the premises to be searched" (International Association of Police, p. 1)

CRIMINAL LAW

Most crimes committed today are crimes because the act is a violation of statutory law. *Statutory law* is law established by legislative bodies, such as the Congress of the United States (Dix and Sharlot, 1987). Most statutory law has its roots embedded deep in the English common law. Common law was based upon judicial precedence, that is, if a case was decided in a particular manner, then it would set a precedent. Common law included major offenses such as homicide, assault, and rape. Two common law offenses were established to protect habitation—burglary and arson. Other common law offenses were crimes against the security of interests in property (Dix and Sharlot, 1987). Robbery, larceny, and extortion would make up this group. Other offenses in English common law covered public health, safety, morals, public authority, and the administration of justice. Today these offenses are made crimes because of statutory law.

Statutory law lists three types of offenses: felonies, misdemeanors, and infractions. Crimes are felonies if the penalty consists of incarceration of more than one year. According to federal law, felonies are ranked by severity of sentence:

Class A—Life in prison

Class B—Twenty-five years

Class C—Twelve years

Class D—Six years

Class E—Three years

These sentences may be accompanied by fines up to $250,000.

Misdemeanors are crimes which require less severe sentences. A misdemeanor involves incarceration of up to, but not to exceed, one year. There are three classes of misdemeanors:

Class A—Up to one year in a jail

Class B—Six months

Class C—One month

Fines may also accompany a misdemeanor sentence. They range from $5,000 to $250,000. The highest fines usually involve a crime where a death occurred.

Infractions are minor violations. They carry a maximum sentence of five days in jail and a maximum fine of $5,000. Most common violations in park backcountry are petty infractions, with fines of $50 to $200.

THE CODE OF FEDERAL REGULATIONS

The passage of laws by Congress does not provide for the implementation of rules and regulations. In the case of the National Park Service, Congress placed the responsibility of implementation with the Secretary of the Interior. The National Park Organic Act of 1916 states that the Secretary shall make such rules and regulations that he may deem necessary for the use and management of the parks. The Code of Federal Regulations are those rules and regulations. The Code of Federal Regulations are divided into fifty chapters or titles. Title 36 of the Code of Federal Regulations governs parks, forests and public lands. These regulations provide for the protection, use and management of persons, property, and natural and cultural resources in areas under the jurisdiction of the National Park Service.

The Code of Federal Regulations is revised each year and issued quarterly. The Office of the Federal Register is responsible for the control and publication of the Code of Federal Regulations. US Code Title 16 laws refer to conservation laws. Title 18 laws refer to criminal actions against the Constitution of the United States. In July of every year, a new code of regulations is published. Title 36 CFR refers to laws that deal with parks, forests, and public property. The NPS enforces these regulations in national parks and the U.S. Forest Service enforces the regulations on national forests and the BLM on other federal public lands.

A compendium is a specific provision (16 US Code section 3, 36 CFR) that concerns individual parks. All National Park Service rangers should be familiar with the 36 Code of Federal Regulations and any special regulations governing the use of their respective parks. These special regulations can be found in a special form called the *Superintendent's Compendium*. A compendium will contain regulations which only apply to a certain park. Some of these compendiums can be found in Section Seven of the 36 Code of Federal Regulations. Be sure to check with your supervisor for any additional regulations which pertain to your park.

The Constitution, in concert with its various amendments and other rules and regulations, forms the framework of our criminal justice system, which includes the national park backcountry ranger. They specify how rangers will protect society from criminal threats while insuring that personal freedoms and liberties are preserved. All rangers must possess a thorough knowledge of these laws and regulations so that they will operate properly in exercising their authority. It is recommended that anyone pursuing a career as a law enforcement ranger study constitutional law.

References

Code of Federal Regulations, *Parks, Forests, and Public Property* (Washington D.C.: Office of the Federal Register National Archives and Records) 1992.

Dix, George E. and M. Michael Sharlot, *Criminal Law* (Minnesota: West Publishing Co.) 1987.

Epstein, Lee and Thomas Walker, *Constitutional Law for a Changing America* (Washington D.C.: C Q Press) 1992.

Federal Law Enforcement Training Center, *NPS Search and Seizure.* (Washington D.C.: Govt. Printing Office) 1984.

Federal Law Enforcement Training Center, *NPS Authority and Jurisdiction Student Guide.* Washington D.C.: Govt. Printing Office) 1980.

Federal Law Enforcement Training Center, *NPS Authority and Jurisdiction.* (Washington D.C. : Govt. Printing Office) 1992.

U.S. Department of the Interior, *NPS-9; Law Enforcement Policy and Guidelines.* Ranger Activities Division, National Park Service (Washington D.C.: Govt. Printing Office) 1989.

CHAPTER *3*

GAINING COMPLIANCE
IN THE BACKCOUNTRY

T he purpose of this chapter is to explain how the intentional violator differs from the unknowing violator. The unknowing violator, if not handled with kindness, can turn into an intentional violator. As will be explained, the ranger is not there to punish behavior, but to correct it.

TYPES OF VIOLATIONS

Gaining compliance is sometimes easier if the ranger first understands the various types of violations and the individuals who commit them. Hendee, Stankey and Lucas (1990), state that these violations can best be understood by first considering a classification of undesirable visitor actions and their impacts. They list five different types of violations. Each will be discussed.

ILLEGAL UNINFORMED ACTIONS

The first type of violation are *illegal uninformed actions.* Examples of these include the use of an off-road vehicle in a designated wilderness area, stealing artifacts, or camping in a clearly marked restricted place. An action such as these would call for a clear law enforcement action. These may also be situations which may call for an educational approach. The violator may not know that he/she is in an area that is designated wilderness. The wrong approach at a particular time may also be inappropriate. Later in this chapter, there will be a discussion concerning the many varied actions law enforcement rangers should and should not take concerning unknowing violators. For now, we shall continue with the typology of violations.

THOUGHTLESS VIOLATIONS

The second type is the *thoughtless violations of regulations.* An example of a thoughtless violation is littering (i.e., someone throws trash on a trail without even thinking that the action is a violation of a law; a boater fails to pay attention to the wake his/her vessel is creating when he/she is approaching a marina harbor). Both examples are violations of the 36 CFR, and both examples could be controlled by the use of persuasion on the part of law enforcement. Litter bags could be given out with the user's backcountry permits. The wake problem could be solved by forcing the boater through a small opening in a floating boom across the entrance to the marina or safe harbor, while at the same time placing the regulatory information on the boom or near it. These actions on the part of the rangers would assure compliance and save the violator an embarrassing contact with law enforcement.

UNSKILLED ACTIONS

The third type is called *unskilled actions*, such as ditching around a tent in a developed campground. Such ditching is a violation of the 36 CFRs. Other violations which could possibly fall under this classification would be failure to properly dispose of human wastes or to urinate upon beaches in areas where it is proper to urinate into the river in order to avoid an uric acid buildup on the shore. Education is the only solution to these types of unskilled actions. Law enforcement rangers must always be conscious of their attitudes and demeanors when approaching violators who have committed these types of offenses.

UNINFORMED BEHAVIOR

The fourth type is uninformed behavior. Hendee, Stankey, and Lucas state that this uninformed behavior can lead to overcrowding of particular areas because large numbers of visitors enter a wilderness at a few well known access points. If they had been better informed, they could have used less crowded entry points and lessened the impact on an area. In order to avoid this type of problem, the visitor must be provided with more information prior to the trip.

UNAVOIDABLE MINIMUM IMPACT

The last type, as listed by Hendee, Stankey and Lucas, is *unavoidable minimum impacts*. Visitors step upon vegetation and compress it under tents and sleeping bags and leave human waste behind in some areas. The accumulation is unavoidable, therefore impact is also unavoidable. Care must be used to prevent excess impact, especially in the backcountry. The only method of eliminating this problem is to eliminate use. This solution would hardly be appropriate in most areas of a park.

UNKNOWING VIOLATORS

This text is most concerned with the first three types of violators. The illegal action or thoughtless violation is often committed by what law enforcement rangers refer to as unknowing violators. Unknowing violators are people who just do not know that they are doing something that is wrong. They may be ignorant of the regulation, they may not be able to read the regulations posted near the trailhead, they may not understand what they did read, they may be afraid that a ranger might think that they were stupid if they asked questions after they received an explanation, or they may be acting out of tradition. In many parts of the country, recreationists have been hunting, fishing, boating, camping or just using a piece of land the same way their fathers and grandfathers and great-grandfathers have. They are simply unaware of the legal changes which may have taken place over the years.

┌───┐

— **Real Life Situation** ─────────

An example of this occurred in Great Basin National Park. Great Basin National Park was only a small National Monument prior to 1987. The park was enlarged by the transfer of National Forest land which surrounded the monument. Much of this property was previously open to hunting. While there is no hunting allowed in a National Park, the traditional use of this land was for hunting. It was difficult to explain to the residents who hunted upon these lands that because of a land ownership change from the National Forest Service to the National Park Service, the land could no longer be used for hunting purposes.

└───┘

EDUCATING THE VISITOR

Education is a hot topic in the wilderness management field. We speak of educating the visitor, educating young people before they visit the backcountry, and educating people in aspects of low impact wilderness use. Most of us use the term *education* in a very generic way. It is one thing to be able to visit a sixth grade classroom and teach all of the children low impact camping, but what about the individuals you stop out in the backcountry of a park with an open campfire above the tree level in a restricted alpine area? How do you educate these individuals? They know that they are in violation; it was clearly posted. They know if they are caught, they will have to pay. They may pay their fine, but I guarantee you that you have not achieved real long term compliance. They will rekindle their fires. It may be on the next trip, but you did not educate or change their behavior with a $25 citation. They considered it part of their trip costs.

THE RESOURCE MESSAGE

We must be prepared to leave a resource message with any and all violators—a message they will understand, one that will gain their compliance, a message that will correct their behavior, not punish them. As law enforcement rangers, we must be like Clint Eastwood in his movie Heartbreak Ridge, we must be ready to improvise, adapt and overcome. This simply means that when we come into contact with the unknowing violator we, like Eastwood, must be ready to improvise, adapt, and overcome in our dealing with the person. If the situation calls for a simple resource message, then give one. If the situation turns ugly and you are confronting an angry huge person, adapt—run if necessary, use defensive tactics, or talk your way out of the situation, but make sure that when the incident is over, you have a compliant individual who will not commit the same violation again. If the incident truly calls for you to overcome the individual and make a physical arrest, then you will have plenty of opportunity to try to educate the individual on your way to the nearest federal holding facility.

GAINING COMPLIANCE

Law enforcement officers understand the meaning of compliance. It means to yield to the request of another. It does not mean to be forced to yield—it is a voluntary act. In the earlier days of park law enforcement, the younger members of the citizenry did not challenge authority. Compliance was gained just by the presence of a law enforcement officer. If Mom or Dad said it was so in the 1940s or 50s, then that was the way it was. If a teacher said it was a certain way, then it was. As we as a society have moved through the 60s, 70s, and 80s, and into the 90s, things have changed. Children in schools learn to challenge authority. There is a button going around, it says, "Question Authority." Is it any wonder that our authority in the parks is questioned? Is it any wonder that we must know how to educate in order to gain compliance? The best part about this change is that once we make the unknowing violator understand why he/she must not commit the violation again, he/she will probably not do it again. Yes, we have gained compliance. In order to effectively do our job of resource and visitor protection, we must educate the unknowing violator. Let us reconceptualize education in this context. Education should be a tool to cure the unknowing violator.

CURING THE UNKNOWING VIOLATOR

Just who is an unknowing violator? An unknowing violator is a person who is unaware they have committed some wrong. For our purposes, that wrong was committed in the backcountry of a national park. They have committed an act which violates a standard of conduct or a standard of behavior. The important thing is that you, as a law enforcement ranger, will intervene. You have the ability to control and direct the individual's behavior. In this particular situation, you will not concern yourself with punishing the violator, it's not your job. Your job is to correct the violator. Punishment is meted out to a guilty person by a court of law. The person in front of you now is innocent. The Constitution states that all are innocent until proven guilty. Therefore, you do not punish the violator, not even a verbal berating. It will not gain compliance! You correct the violator. You do not have the right or authority to punish. The result you want is compliance. You gain compliance with the proper attitude and demeanor along with a resource message to fit the situation. Occasionally you will have to resort to additional means, but remember improvise, adapt and overcome.

ATTITUDE REINFORCEMENT

Law enforcement rangers must understand the resource that they are protecting and its value. You would not be reading this book if the resource were of no value to you. The unknowing violator will never think of the resources in the same manner as we do. They do not think about them; they take them for granted. To them, its just there, they use it and abuse it. The environment is going to suck it up anyway, so just toss it on the ground. You and

I understand about biodegradable products, we know that some items will not disintegrate and disappear. The unknowing violator does not know that it will be there forever. That is the important point that I want you to remember. You and I know, they do not know!! How can we make them aware of these things? We must educate the unknowing violator in order to cure them.

UNDERSTANDING THE VIOLATOR

Why is the unknowing violator uneducated? Why are they unknowing? Because they have a lack of information. How many of these people stop at the ranger station before venturing out in the backcountry? They may only stop if it is mandatory to pick up a backcountry permit, and he/she is usually the person who has all the answers and never asks questions of the ranger behind the desk. We really need to require these folks to listen to a presentation of the important rules and regulations along with an explanation of why the rules and regulations are being implemented.

ATTITUDE

I have heard rangers say, " I am not going out there and educate those people, I am going to cite and arrest them." This does not solve the problem. Without education and information we will never achieve compliance. All law enforcement rangers should be required to take an interpretation course in order to give them more available tools in order to achieve compliance. There is no room in the National Park Service for the guy with a bad attitude. This type of ranger will never gain compliance from the unknowing violator. If a person is treated with kindness, you will be more likely to receive the same treatment in return. If you approach an unknowing violator with a belligerent attitude and demeanor, assuredly you will receive similar treatment. There was an informal survey conducted in Oklahoma among state troopers (Johnson). The survey asked the troopers, "What is the major criteria, or what do you utilize or think about, when you write a citation for an offense?" Ninety-seven percent of the troopers responding answered that it depended upon the violators attitude. The violator's attitude! What about the officer's attitude? If the officer changed her/his demeanor, wouldn't it change the violators demeanor too? We must also educate the adult recreationist. When they venture out in the environment, be it wilderness or other backcountry areas, we must be ready to educate them about the proper use of these areas. We must become involved with these people and get them involved with the environment.

We must avoid having a negative attitude at all costs. A ranger who walks up to a visitor who is in violation, may think that the violator is "bad." The ranger might be right but how is that going to affect the visitor? What sort of image does this type of attitude create in your mind. It is the negative image of a macho cop. Rangers are not cops. We are reminded that we are there for visitor and resource protection. The unknowing violator must be educated. The process can not begin with a negative attitude. The ranger must overcome these attitudinal barriers. There can not be a free flow of ideas and communication between the officer and the visitor if such barriers exist.

BODY LANGUAGE

Communication is the transmittal of information in many modes—verbal and non verbal. A ranger can, without saying one word, transmit a message such as "I have your ticket right here dirt bag." Does this body language gain compliance? No!

Can you teach or educate the visitor with your hands? Definitely. It is another form of nonverbal communication. If you exit your patrol cruiser or get off of your horse and motion vehemently with your hands, what kind of message are you communicating to the unknowing violator? The person is likely to become upset and agitated before they even know what violation they have committed. It would be better to wave at the person in a friendly manner and approach in a friendly casual walk in order to prepare their attitude for a meaningful resource message concerning their particular violation.

Would you use a four letter vernacular directed toward a violator. If you even think in those terms it may be communicated to the person through your demeanor. That is a power play. It is an authoritarian act. You do have the authority to restrict a persons freedom and to "punish" them. But that is not your job. It is your job to gain compliance, in order to protect the visitor and the resource. Thoughts of four letter vernaculars prohibit the flow of positive communication between the violator and officer. Think about your objective—to gain compliance and to correct behavior, not to punish! The person may say "I didn't know," he/she probably didn't. Its your job to educate them.

WHAT IF?

We all know that the simplest violator can turn ugly and threaten our existence. That is why we must always be prepared. When I say have a positive attitude, I am not telling you to forgo caution and prudence. The Chief Ranger at Glen Canyon National Recreation Area, Larry Clark, has an acronym that best fits all of what I have been telling you into a neat package. The acronym is RHOMP, no it does not mean to rhomp over the visitor. It means to "R", treat everyone you come into contact with, the same way you would want to be treated, with respect. "H", to be honest in your dealings with the visitor. Do not tell him lies or make threats. Be up front and honest. "O", be objective. Do not become subjective and take the violation the person committed as a personal affront. Treat all people the same, be objective in the manner in which you treat the unknowing or knowing violator. "M", be moral. Do not lecture visitors on the evil of their ways and go out and do the same things after you are through with work for the day. No one appreciates or believes a ranger for long if they do not practice what they preach. "P" is for prudence. Be prudent in all your approaches. If something does not feel right about a certain violation or violator or if there are too many visitors for one ranger to safely approach, be prudent and back off and wait for help to arrive. Know when to back off and know when to run. Be prudent!

The first thing that is going to happen when you make your appearance is that both you and the violator will form a perception of each other. Are you both to become four letter vernaculars? If that is the way you perceive an individual then according to your values that is what the person will become. You may not perceive a person as being good unless their behavior demonstrates something favorable. In my example of the fishing violator, you see someone committing a violation, fishing illegally. You must establish a favorable relationship to correct their behavior. Ask if the fish are biting. Then suggest that they are biting elsewhere and tell the violator that fishing is not allowed in this particular location. Explain why it is not allowed. Tell the violator about certain spawning habits of the particular species that inhabit these waters and how too much fishing pressure will hurt their populations. Show the violator where a better spot is located and how to get there. If you feel a citation is appropriate, depending on the situation, go ahead and issue it but make sure that your decision is based upon objective information and not on your subjective feelings concerning the violator's attitude.

How do you tell if the person is honestly unknowing about the legality of fishing in that location? Perhaps, the person intentionally violated the law. The person could be lying to you. The person you have approached may not know what they are going to do until they do it. This could be the moment that you have approached an unbalanced individual. This particular moment could be the time that the unknowing violator becomes the intentional violator that you have surprised in the act. Now what? It could turn out to be that one bad incident if you were unprepared. This calls for the "what if" game. I consistently remind the rangers I teach to play the what if game or practice potential scenarios in their minds to be prepared. As you approach the violator ask yourself, what if this person is armed and turns violent? Be prepared for those instances, always, but do not treat every person you encounter with a negative attitude waiting for that one violent individual. Make sure that you have a contingency plan for every potential event. Do not be caught off guard. It is good practice to think of resource messages before you have to give them, just as it is good practice to think of what defensive tactic to use before you approach a potential suspect.

POSITIVE APPROACH

The next most important element in a backcountry ranger's attitude is to be professional in all your daily efforts. If you take professional pride in how you conduct all your contacts, the attitude will be reflected back at you from the unknowing violator. It will become a positive experience, a learning experience.

The first thing that occurs in the curing cycle is awareness. The violator becomes aware of your presence. They have seen you make your arrival. They know something is wrong. It is up to you to make this a positive experience. It all starts upon your greeting and approach. I like to wave and say good morning or afternoon. If I am approaching an individual who is fishing in an illegal place, I always ask how's the fishing? I would never begin with what the hell are you doing fishing here? It establishes all the wrong rapport. Yes, we have the authority to cite and arrest but this will probably not prevent a reoccurrence or educate the individual. It will cause a feeling of animosity. I am not saying that an arrest or citation will not be issued, but the situation should always be a positive experience. Once in a while you will be left with no other choice but to arrest. This is where we have to remember how to improvise, adapt and overcome.

MORE ON COMMUNICATION

Some rangers have excellent communication skills, others do not interface well with the visitor. The backcountry is not the place for rangers with poor communication skills. Surprised? You shouldn't be. The backcountry ranger needs excellent interpersonal communication skills, more so than the frontcountry ranger. The frontcountry ranger can pick up a radio and call for assistance if he/she fouls up an incident with a visitor or violator. The backcountry ranger, whom everyone romanticizes as a loner, an outdoors person who wants to be far away from people, needs to have better communication skills because that ranger can not call for immediate backup. The backcountry ranger must deal with whatever situation they encounter and be able to handle it no matter what the outcome. This ranger better be able to communicate with the violator and make the violator, unknowing or otherwise, understand that he must comply with the regulations. The ranger must also do it in such a way that the violator's behavior is corrected. How can one ranger correct the behavior of a rowdy group of drunk campers 40 miles from the closest trail head? Call for a helicopter full of rangers? Its not always that easy. Good communication skills and knowledge of how to educate people, coupled with masking skills and practiced "what ifs," will usually be the winning combination. The ranger usually does not have the luxury of a backup team in a helicopter, he/she must handle the situation alone.

— **Real Life Situation** ————

Chief Ranger Bruce Edmonston from Craters of the Moon National Monument related this incident to me concerning some rough looking "bikers" he encountered as a ranger in Sequoia Kings Canyon National Park.

Bruce received a complaint about two "bikers" fighting over a female companion in one of his campgrounds. He sought the individuals out. Upon his encounter, he discovered that the individuals were on probation for some serious felonies. He also discovered that these individuals were packing firearms. The firearms were visible. Bruce knew that these particular individuals were potential threats. He also knew that help was far away. He talked to the individuals. He explained to them that he knew that they were on probation. He told them that possessing firearms in a national park was prohibited by the 36 Code of Federal Regulations 2.4 (a)1 (i). Bruce told them that in addition to violating Park Service rules they were also in violation of their probation. Bruce related to these individuals the purpose of national parks. They are a place for the enjoyment of all the people, including them. People needed to feel safe in a Park Service campground. Firearms made other campers feel threatened and fear-ful. Bruce asked them if they wanted to scare other campers with small children and older folks. The bikers replied that they only wanted to enjoy the beauty and serenity of this place too. Bruce asked them for their weapons, and told them that they could pick them up at the ranger station on their way out of the park. He also said that he would not report them to their probation officer. The three individuals were permitted to remain, and they did give Bruce their weapons. Bruce related to me that they were exemplary campers all weekend; no one complained again.

Did Bruce do something wrong by not reporting the firearms violation to the probation office? What about his failure to cite for the weapons violation in the park? Remember that Bruce did gain compliance. The individuals did not have their weapons in the park. The confrontation was ended because of Bruce's verbal skills. The individuals now understood that firearms and fighting were not allowed in the park. They did not violate any park violations that weekend. Bruce accomplished his task of main-taining order in a backcountry campground. He did not sustain any injuries due to a violent confrontation, neither did he have the need to call a backup team to his aid. Bruce used his interpersonal communication skills and his personal awareness to quell what could have been a nasty situation. Bruce gave those individuals a quick lesson about the national parks . Its not an easy task to teach people, let alone to teach unknowing violators.

— **Real Life Situation** ————————

People are all different; they also learn in different ways. I approached an individual who was maintaining a small cooking fire on a beach on Lake Roosevelt. Lake Roosevelt is part of the Coulee Dam National Recreation Area. Beach fires are prohibited on the lake. The first thing out of this individual's mouth after I informed him that fires were not allowed was, "Can't you see, that I was just cooking supper?" "Can't you see that I was not having a campfire?" This is a visual person, a person who perceives his environment through his sense of sight, not his sense of hearing. This type of individual is not going to learn about the dangers of maintaining a campfire just because he hears me tell him its illegal. It just so happened that the area where he was preparing dinner was also the scene of a 250 acre burn from the year before. I pointed at the area directly above us and explained that a campfire caused that fire. The individual looked up and the look on his face changed. He visualized what an illegal fire caused once before. He could see the resource damage caused by an illegal campfire. I educated that individual and gained compliance. In that particular situation, I also issued the person a citation for the fire. He was aware of the ban on beach fires and had deliberately violated the law. The most important fact, though, was that the individual finally saw why fires were not permitted on the beaches of the Coulee Dam National Recreation Area.

Other folks learn best by touching or feeling an object. If that person was this type of learner, perhaps I could have taken him for a walk through the burned over area. I could have had him feel the charred bark of a 100-year-old Ponderosa pine and pick up the charred remains of a furry woodland creature. If that is what is necessary to instruct the unknowing violator, then do it. Some people do just as well when they are taught verbally and hear that they have violated a regulation or law. Find out who you are dealing with and act accordingly. It is not difficult if you pay attention to the person you have encountered. If you do not pay close attention to the individual you have encountered, you may possibly find yourself in a precarious predicament. Pay attention and act prudently.

MASKING

I briefly mentioned the art of masking in the previous section. *Masking* is a psychological term which simply means to be a different person for different situations. A situation occurred a couple of years ago in a national park in which a chief ranger was involved.

— Real Life Situation ————————

The situation involved a group of about 75 intoxicated campers. A ranger was dispatched to that campground to handle the commotion. The ranger was a good law enforcement officer, only he had a John Wayne complex, "an attitude." He walked into the situation like Custer at his last stand. When the chief ranger arrived at the campground, John Wayne was surrounded by hostile, intoxicated campers. It had the makings of a rotten situation, perhaps Stoneman Meadows all over again. The ranger notified his

---

dispatcher about the situation, and the dispatcher notified the chief ranger. The chief arrived with more rangers and stationed them in the shadows where they would not be seen, he then walked into the situation by himself. The crowd started to murmur. Another tough guy ranger was here to stop all of them from having a good time. That is not the impression that the chief ranger gave this group. He put on a real show. The chief was wearing his "silly, effeminate" mask. He walked into that crowd and pretended that he was gay. He waved at the men with a limp wrist and said, "How are all of you gentlemen this evening?" All of those macho intoxicated individuals are starting to mutter, "Hey, this ranger is 'queer.'" The chief had put on a real act to save a potentially bad situation from turning more sour. The chief went on and told the group that they were just going to have to gather up their little things and move along because, "My little ranger friend is just not having a good day." " Please try not to disturb the other campers, pleeeaase boys." Ranger "John Wayne" was really steaming as the "silly" chief ranger grabbed him by the arm and said, "Come on Billy, we have things to do," and they strolled casually out of the melee. The group was just loving it; they could only concentrate on the fact that the chief ranger was effeminate, and they completely forgot about any confrontation that was once on their minds. What happened here?

The chief ranger resorted to rather extraordinary means to possibly save the life of the ranger who had escalated the situation to near violence. He had also corrected the group's behavior and gained compliance. The group broke up and actually left the campground laughing about the chief ranger. If it gains compliance and corrects behavior while still within the legal and moral confines of the law then try it.

CONCLUSION

Remember the adage from Clint Eastwood's movie, improvise, adapt and overcome. If the chief approached this group and spoke to them in authoritative manner, there would have been no compliance, and someone would probably have suffered injuries and the court system would have incurred a huge increase in additional cases. Competent law enforcement, especially in the backcountry demands expertise in an internal power. That power is interpersonal communication, the ability to persuade. You must be able to persuade people to comply without bending them into submission through the formal powers of arrest. This is how the unknowing violator must be dealt with.

CHAPTER *4*

NATURAL RESOURCE LAWS

T his chapter will illustrate how federal regulations were established to provide protection for all creatures, plants, and resources which make up the park environment. We will discuss how existing laws became laws, and we will explore the various methods which are used to investigate violations of these laws. We will end this chapter with a discussion concerning the impacts illegal activities have on populations, genetic viability and on the integrity of the ecosystem.

Some of the specific laws and regulations we will examine are:

- The Bald Eagle Act 16 USC 433

- The Lacey Act 18 USC 43

- The National Environmental Policy Act (42USC 4321, 4331 to 4335, 4341 to 4347 PL 91-190)

- The Endangered Species Act 16 USC 668

- The Wilderness Act (16USC 1131 to 1136 PL 88-577)

- The Wild Free-Roaming Horse and Burros Protection Act (16USC 1338)

- The Airborne Hunting Statute 16USC 742 j-1

- The Migratory Bird Treaty Act 16 USC 701 et seq

59

THE BALD EAGLE ACT

The Bald Eagle Act (16 USC 668) prohibits the taking, possessing, selling, purchase, barter, transport, export, or import of any part, alive or dead, or a portion of the nest or egg of a Bald Eagle or Golden Eagle. This basically states that you cannot possess or deal in anything that involves Bald or Golden Eagles.

The penalties can be either criminal or civil. The criminal penalties for violating this law are $5,000 and/or one year imprisonment for the first conviction; $10,000 and/or two years imprisonment for the second and any subsequent convictions. A person may also be taken to civil court for violating this act. Most of these cases involve livestock and grazing permits in the western portions of our country. Stockmen may shoot at eagles which, in their consideration, may be killing or injuring stock which belongs to them. A finding against the stockmen in civil court may involve damages up to $5,000 for each incident. It could also involve the cancellation of any grazing permits with land management agencies. The forfeiture of any animal parts and all guns, traps, and equipment, as well as vehicles used to aid in the violation is also a possibility.

— Real Life Situation ——————————

A law enforcement ranger does not take the Eagle Act lightly. I received a report concerning eagle parts which were discovered near a little used campsite on Lake Roosevelt. I investigated the report and discovered the remains of a bald eagle. It had apparently died of natural causes. I gathered up the remains and they were handed over to the Indian museum under the control of a local Native American tribal government. The Native Americans are issued permits which entitle them to possess eagle parts.

THE LACEY ACT

The Lacey Act was originally passed in 1900. Its purpose was to outlaw interstate traffic in birds and other animals illegally killed in the state of their origin. It initially targeted the market hunter (i.e., the individual who killed huge quantities of game to sell on the open market). The Lacey Act is a federal tool which helps the state enforce their own conservation laws. The Black Bass Act was virtually the same as the Lacey Act except it involved the illegal trafficking in fish. They were combined in 1981. No statute has proved to be as effective as the Lacey Act in combating wildlife violations. This law protects fish, wildlife and rare plants by providing more effective enforcement of state, federal, Indian tribal and foreign conservation laws (Lacey Act Amendments of 1981, PL 97-79). In order for a ranger to charge an individual with a violation under the Lacey Act, it must first be proven that there has been a violation of an underlying law relating to fish, plants or wildlife. An example of this would be the apprehension of individuals in the Great Smoky Mountains National Park for killing black bears. They have violated the 36 CFRs section 2.2 (a) (1), which states that the taking of animals in a park is prohibited except by authorized hunting and trapping activities. The individuals in this park were also taking the bear parts and selling them to an oriental dealer in another section of the country. This person would then ship the parts to the Far East. The individuals involved were charged with a violation under the Lacey Act because the parts were shipped by way of interstate commerce.

The Lacey Act prohibits the import, export, transportation of, selling, buying, etc., of any fish, wildlife or plant taken or possessed in violation of any law, treaty or regulation of the United States or tribal law. This also includes any jurisdiction within the special maritime and territories of the United States as specified by Section 7 of title 18 USC.

The penalties for violating this act include a $10,000 maximum fine imposed as damages in civil court and a maximum of $20,000 and/or five years for a knowing violation, or $10,000 and/or one year for unknowing violations. There is also a forfeiture clause which accompanies this law, in addition to the suspension of federal hunting and fishing rights.

THE AIR-BORNE HUNTING STATUTE

The Air Borne Hunting Statute was initially passed in 1956 and amended in 1972 (PL92-502). The law was passed to protect birds, fish and wildlife from harassment by aircraft. It prohibited the shooting, or attempts to shoot, for the purpose of taking or capturing birds, fish and wildlife.

The law was specifically aimed at violations by commercial big game outfitters and those who would heard flocks or herds of animals for the purpose of market hunting. The most common violations today occur in areas such as Wrangell St. Elias National Park and Preserve where outfitted big game hunts are permitted in portions of the reserve and park. Some unscrupulous outfitters do anything to guarantee their clients a trophy animal, including spotting it, herding it, and even shooting it from an airplane.

The penalties for violating this law are criminal and include a $5,000 fine and/or one year in jail. It may also include forfeiture, suspension of hunting rights and or permits, and even confiscation of guns and aircraft.

THE MIGRATORY BIRD TREATY ACT

The Migratory Bird Treaty Act (16 USC 701 et seq) makes the killing, taking, or possessing of migratory birds unlawful unless such taking is authorized by such regulations provided for in other sections of the act. This also includes the importing or exporting of feathers and parts.

The act was initiated in 1916 as a treaty with Great Britain. It later included treaties with Japan and the United Mexican States. Section 704 of the act determines how and when migratory birds may be taken or killed (Title 16 USC sec. 704). This section states how regulations can establish seasons. The penalties for violating this act are as follows: a $500 fine and/or six months in jail for a noncommercial violation; $2,000 fine and/or two years in prison for a commercial violation of the law. All items used in such a taking are subject to forfeiture.

THE ENDANGERED SPECIES ACT

The Endangered Species Act (16 USC 1538 et seq) is a law which commits us, as a nation, to protecting plants and animals from extinction. The Endangered Species Act states that in order to protect a species, we must conserve the species' genetic diversity. We do this by protecting subspecies and even distinct individual populations. An example would be the protection being offered to the Northern Spotted Owl in the Pacific Northwest.

This act has just one simple objective—the recovery of that particular species to the point where its continuation as a species is no longer in question. The act is divided into two sections or prongs:

1) The law lists species and their critical habitat.

2) It provides protection for both. According to Cubbage, O'Laughlin and Bullock, at the end of March 1991, there were 360 U.S. animal species, 246 U.S. plant species and 522 foreign species listed as endangered by the U.S. Fish and Wildlife Service. The manner of protection offered to these species is provided by three main prohibitions. These prohibitions are:

√   Trade in endangered species is prohibited except by permit. Permits are rare and difficult to attain.

√   No one may take an endangered species, this could mean to kill, or to destroy its habitat, or to harass the animal.

√   Actions on the part of federal agencies must not jeopardize a species or its habitat.

A prime example of the importance of the Endangered Species Act to the National Park Service is the species of desert tortoise which is found in the Lake Mead National Recreation Area. The desert tortoise was responsible for the cancellation of a large marina project considered by the National Park Service. The species was found in the area, and the habitat would have been severely affected by any construction. The survey could not even be completed because of the impact on the tortoise's habitat.

Violations of the Endangered Species Act may be prosecuted as a criminal activity. It carries a criminal penalty of $20,000 and/ or one year imprisonment. It also has a civil penalty attached. It consists of a fine of $5,000 for each violation. As with the other laws, it contains a forfeiture clause.

THE WILDERNESS ACT

The Wilderness Act of 1964 became law after 66 modifications and resubmissions and over eight years of debate. The original act designated 9.1 million acres as wilderness. The Wilderness Act gave authority to Congress, not the land management agencies or the president, to declare an appropriate area as wilderness. *Wilderness* is defined as "an area where the earth and its community of life are untrammeled by man, where man himself is a visitor and does not remain." (Wilderness Act of 1964, 16 USC 1131 to 1136). The Wilderness Act provides many prohibitions. No motorized conveyances may be operated or brought into such an area. No wheeled conveyances are allowed. In some wilderness areas, planes are not allowed to fly lower than 3,000 feet . There are regulations which are special for each area also. Some of these violations may be misdemeanors, while others are felonies. Check with the agency in charge of the particular area.

Subsequent acts provide for the inclusion of areas which are much smaller than originally considered for inclusion into the wilderness system. This was passed to allow for inclusion of regrown properties in the eastern United States.

THE **1969** NATIONAL ENVIRONMENTAL POLICY ACT **(NEPA)**

Any federal actions which occur on federal lands or are paid for with federal funding are required to be preceded by an environmental impact analysis. According to Cubbage, O'Laughlin and Bullock (1993), the environmental assessment or EA is the initial document necessary for planning and decision making. It is used to show whether a proposed project would have significant impact on the quality of the human environment. If the action would have considerable impact, then an Environmental Impact Statement (EIS) must be prepared to ensure compliance with NEPA. If no impact was found by the Environmental Assessment, then an EIS would not be prepared. A finding of *No Significant Impact* would be drafted for public review.

All projects considered by the National Park Service must go through this process. Constructing campgrounds, trails, concession buildings and even reintroduction of species long absent from certain areas must go through the NEPA process before approval is given for the project.

THE WILD FREE-ROAMING HORSE AND BURROS ACT OF **1971**

This act was designed to protect wild horses and burros as a symbol of our western heritage. It also served the humanitarian purpose to protect individual animals from being brutalized and sold for pet food. The act made the animals an important part of the natural system (Cubbage, O'Laughlin and Bullock).

The act made it a crime to kill or take wild horses and burros from public lands. The act has been challenged in the Supreme Court, and an important ruling has come forth. The Supreme Court has affirmed the power of the federal government to control all wildlife species on the lands under its control. This includes lands controlled by the National Park Service. The case in which this was decided was *Kleppe v. New Mexico* (426 US 529 [1976]). Prior to this ruling, the federal government depended upon the state game laws to govern wildlife populations on federal land. The act has remained the center of a large controversy concerning what to do with the ever increasing herds of wild horses and burros in the western portions of the United States.

THE EVOLUTION OF FEDERAL NATURAL RESOURCE LAWS

Farsighted individuals, as early as the 1830s, saw the necessity for national laws which would protect and preserve the environment. George Catlin called for the formation of National Parks in 1832. Yellowstone was saved for all people to enjoy in 1872. Individuals, such as Theodore Roosevelt, Gifford Pinchot, John Muir, Aldo Leopold, Bob Marshall, Howard Zahniser and others, all saw the need to do something to protect our resources and our environment from being destroyed by overuse and neglect. Without their efforts, this text would be unnecessary because there would be no backcountry to protect or visitors to visit.

The passage of these national laws enables National Park rangers to better perform their protection duties. The laws give us the authority we need to protect the environment from misuse, both from outside the agency and from within the agency.

A brief look at the evolution of federal laws takes us from the establishment of Yellowstone National Park in 1872, Yosemite in 1890, to the passage of the Lacey Act in 1900. The Lacey Act enabled the federal government to better support state game laws and to give additional protection to vulnerable species. Theodore Roosevelt was responsible for bringing millions of acres into the protection of the federal government, much to the consternation of many state's rights advocates. Further actions protected migratory birds from mass extinction from market hunters, and the Wilderness Act brought millions of more wild acres under federal protection. Today the environment, while still not protected to the degree many of us would prefer, is protected better than it would have been without federal control.

NATURAL RESOURCE INVESTIGATORY PROCEDURES

Extensive investigations concerning natural resource law violations are conducted in order to collect legal evidence that will reveal the method used to commit the crime. The evidence gathered in such investigations will establish the *corpus delicti* of the crime. In other words, it will include the elements needed in order to prove a crime has been committed.

The first step is to investigate the crime scene. This includes the recognition of what is evidence, the protection of that evidence, the collection of the evidence, and the identification and preservation of that evidence. Finally, officers must maintain the chain of custody of that evidence. It is important to understand that the investigation of these types of crimes is just as complex as the investigation of serious common law crimes. The National Laboratory maintained by the Federal Bureau of Investigation may be employed as well as the resources of the U.S. Fish and Wildlife Service, state crime labs and various resources found in colleges and universities. What follows is an example of a complex investigation. The participating agency or the individuals involved will not be revealed.

— Real Life Situation ———————————

While on a regular wilderness patrol of an area located in a western state, a ranger discovered the remains of three wild horses, or what he believed to be wild horses. He immediately determined that the area must be cordoned off, just in case someone else would stumble upon the area as he did and destroy evidence. The ranger did this by stretching marking tape around the immediate area and fastening it down with rocks. He took photos of the carcasses and found large truck tracks and tracks from a road grader. This area was along a stretch of road that bordered a wilderness study area. He also found seven used 30:06 cartridges near the tracks. The officer photographed all of this evidence and made a cast of the track he found. Upon further investigation he located an individual in a nearby town who told him that there was a sportsman's club which consisted of individuals who thought the wild horses were adversely affecting the local wild game populations. Some of these individuals worked for the local county as road repair workers. The ranger obtained a search warrant based upon this testimony and the physical evidence which he gathered at the scene. With this warrant, he compared the cast taken at the scene to the large trucks and graders in the county's equipment lot. The officer was able to look for a weapon which matched the cartridges he found. The evidence matched the tread of one truck and grader in that lot. The ranger also found a rifle of the same calibre in the truck. It did not take much further investigation to identify the individuals who operated that equipment. The carcasses were sent to the laboratories of a university and forensic tests were run to determine the cause of death. The cause of death was attributed to the gun shot wounds found upon the carcasses. The slugs were sent to the FBI's ballistic division and compared to the rifling and bullets fired from the confiscated weapon, another match. The castings and the tire treads were also analyzed by the state crime lab. The ranger arrested the individuals involved and charged them with a felony under the Wild and Free-Roaming Horse and Burro's Act of 1971. The individuals were convicted and sentenced to probation and a fine.

NEGATIVE IMPACTS TO THE ENVIRONMENT BY COMMERCIAL ACTIVITIES

The most blatant negative impacts to our environment by commercial activities are caused by the mining industry. According to Peter Nigh, a Park Service instructor at the Albright Training Center in Arizona, mining also refers to the exploration and mining of oil, gas and coal, covered by the Mineral Leasing Act of 1920. The demand for these fossil fuels is having negative impacts upon the adjacent park lands, near the mining areas and the energy generating plants themselves. Coal-fired generators, such as the Navajo Plant located in Utah, discharge particulate contaminates into the airshed over many western National Parks. The water used to cool these units is flushed into the natural water table and eventually contaminates the reservoirs surrounded by national recreation areas such as Glen Canyon. There are now two important means of controlling these discharges which have the potential for impacting national parks—the Clean Air Act and the Federal Water Pollution Control Act.

Negative impacts can result from exploration as well as discharge. Exploratory drilling has opened up millions of acres of land adjoining the national park system. These exploratory roads make available all of these previously inaccessible areas to off-road vehicle enthusiasts. This will disturb previously undisturbed wildlife populations and wild ecosystems and is bound to transform backcountry into frontcountry.

We must truly remain committed to our mission. To preserve and to protect our parks for now and for future generations to enjoy.

References

Cubbage, Fredrick, Jay O'Laughlin and Charles Bullock, *Forest Resource Policy* (New York: John Wiley and Sons) 1993.

CHAPTER 5

ARREST AND DETENTION
IN THE BACKCOUNTRY

T he purpose of this chapter is to aid the potential backcountry ranger in identifying the elements of a lawful arrest. It will provide the guidelines for the determination of probable cause and the various legal aspects of detention and interrogation. Backcountry arrest procedures are outlined.

HISTORY OF ARREST

Before the time of the conquest of England by William of Normandy, the private citizen bore all of the responsibility of arresting criminals and keeping the peace. After the Norman conquest, the government began to take over the responsibilities of arrest and detention.

The common law concept was brought to America and with it came the powers of arrest for government agents. An arrest for a misdemeanor could be made if it was committed in the presence of an agent or officer. Warrantless arrests for felonies could be made as long as the officer had probable cause, regardless of whether the act was observed by the officer. The "presence" requirement is an extension of a belief that if the act did not occur in the officer's presence, then the arrest is not based on his direct observation; therefore, a warrant should be obtained. The magistrate, being a neutral, objective individual shall decide, upon the basis of the probable cause presented, if a warrant should be issued. Felonies are a threat to the public good, and the risk involved with harm to the public outweighs the danger concerning warrantless arrests. Today, statutes have modified the common law rule and permit warrantless arrests for both misdemeanors and felonies based upon probable cause and not on observation alone.

Even though modern statutes have changed the warrantless requirement, backcountry and frontcountry rangers must still follow common law. This has been codified in Title 16 USC 1a - 6. It states that rangers will only arrest in their presence or with a warrant for a misdemeanor. A ranger may arrest a person for a felony with probable cause or upon a warrant (NPS-9). The individual must have been identified as having committed that felony. If you have the time to obtain a warrant, then obtain one!

ORGANIC ACT OF 1916

The Organic Act of 1916 (Title 16 USC 1a-6) gave arrest authority to National Park Service employees. Before Title 16 USC 1a - 6, the National Park Service operated under a variety of vague statutes going back to common law. The Organic Act, as approved by the House Committee of Interior and Insular Affairs, gave designated personnel of the National Park Service the authority to make arrests, to bear firearms, and to enforce all federal laws. The actions of law enforcement in the National Park Service ranks flow through the General Authorities Act of 1976. The NPS must also keep up-to-date with Supreme Court Decisions.

Arrest procedures for national park rangers are also provided for in the NPS-9. As discussed earlier, these are the National Park Service's guidelines for law enforcement. They were originated by the Park Service in 1975 and updated in 1984. As far as the National Park Service is concerned, NPS-9 is another source of law. All law enforcement rangers must adhere to and utilize the guidelines set forth in the NPS-9.

ARREST

Arrest is the legal authority necessary to apprehend and to detain an individual in order that the person be made to answer for an alleged crime or offense (FLETC, 1992). It is possible to violate a person's civil rights by arresting them without formally doing so. Officers must use extreme caution in such situations. Arrests are sometimes made without the officer being aware of the fact that he/she has just arrested a person. A ranger could be walking through a campground asking questions about a "Peeping Tom" looking into various tents in the campground. The ranger could actually be effecting an arrest. If the particular individual you stop and question feels compelled to stand there with you and is afraid to leave until you are finished, it could be considered an arrest. Your own words can be detaining. Be careful how you question or stop a person. Make sure that if you do not intend to arrest an individual, they know that they are free to leave at anytime.

The authority a law enforcement ranger has to enact an arrest comes from (Title 16 USC 1a-6), the General Authorities Act of 1976. This authority allows National Park Service rangers to carry firearms, make arrests without warrants if an offense is committed in the ranger's presence, or arrest for a felony recognizable under federal law (PL 94-458). The General Authorities Act of 1976 actually repealed the old authority from the National Park Service Organic Act and provided the rangers new authority to enforce the laws. The General Authorities Act (16 USC 1a-6) clarifies authority as follows:

> In addition to any other authority conferred by law, the Secretary of the Interior is authorized to designate... certain officers or employees of the Department of the Interior... In performance of such duties...May:"

> 1. Carry firearms and make arrests without warrant for any offense against the United States committed in his presence, or for any felony cognizable under the laws of the United States if he has reasonable grounds to believe that the person to be arrested has committed or is committing such felony, provided such arrests occur within that system or the person to be arrested is fleeing to avoid arrest.

2. Execute any warrant or other process issued by a court or officer of competent jurisdiction for the enforcement of the provisions of any federal law or regulation issued pursuant to law arising out of an offense in that system or where the person subject to the warrant or process is in that system, in connection with any federal offense.

3. Conduct investigations of offenses against the United States committed in that system in the absence of investigation thereof by any other federal law enforcement agency having investigative jurisdiction over the offense committed or with the concurrence of such other agency."

Felony arrests may be undertaken when the offense has occurred outside of the officer's presence as long as the ranger has sufficient probable cause that the person committed the offense.

Law enforcement rangers can also execute warrants and other processes, such as a summons, issued by the court for the enforcement of federal laws or regulations. The "paper" can be served outside of the park for offenses committed within the system.

WARRANTLESS ARRESTS

As stated above, these arrests can be effected if they occur in the ranger's presence. This includes the use of all senses. If you hear, see, feel or smell a crime taking place, then you can arrest the offender. This also includes special aids which enhance the ranger's senses. An example can be binoculars or electronic listening devices, which amplify sounds. One thing to remember is that the misdemeanor arrest must be made without unreasonable delay. You cannot see an offense being committed, leave, and come back the next day and arrest the individual for a misdemeanor. This may be possible if it is a felony because you may need to establish probable cause before you arrest. A reasonable delay is acceptable if you are awaiting backup before making an arrest.

In Glacier National Park, individuals are not put under physical arrest when they are initially encountered in the backcountry. The ranger escorts the individual out to a trail or road where the ranger can access a vehicle. It is at that point that the person is placed under arrest by the ranger. The person is hand-cuffed and transported to the closest federal holding facility. The reason for this procedure is visitor safety and ranger liability. The ranger is responsible for the individual's well-being until the person is placed in the holding facility. The ranger is advised in Glacier not to arrest until proper procedures can be followed (Roger Semler, 1993 Glacier NP).

PROBABLE CAUSE

Probable cause was defined in chapter two, but I believe it is important enough to repeat in a chapter about arrest and detention.

> Probable cause exists where the facts and circumstances within the officer's knowledge of which they had reasonable, trustworthy information, are sufficient in themselves to warrant a man of reasonable caution in the belief that an offense has been or is being committed. *Brinegar v. United States* 338 U.S. 160, 1949

The more a ranger can tie in the facts of an offense to the probable cause, the better a U.S. Magistrate will like it. For example, never state that the color of a suspect's coat or backpack made you suspicious. Always articulate your exact reasons. A detailed description of a potential suspect, as well as being able to place the person at the scene of the crime at approximately the right time may be enough probable cause to effect an arrest. An important point to remember is that a ranger can be cross-examined in court to find out if the ranger used questioning, suspicion, or investigation in order to detain an individual prior to establishing sufficient probable cause. Two requirements are necessary for probable cause: a crime must have been committed and you must have some cause to believe that the person you arrested committed the crime. You may be wrong, but as long as you have adequate probable cause you are free of liability. This is called *good faith immunity*.

There are two ways to get information to establish probable cause: (1) From the perception of the officer's five senses. The officer is given credence because of the officer's personal expertise. The crime may have been committed in the officer's presence. (2) Other factors act as indications of criminal activity, these can support probable cause (e.g., flight; physical or real evidence; furtive conduct; admissions; the finding of a suspect at the scene of a crime; the personal association with a criminal element; a past criminal record; facts uncovered by an investigation; false or implausible answers). These activities are not enough to establish probable cause by themselves unless it is corroborated with physical evidence or personal observation. You must string together several facts to establish probable cause.

The preference of the U.S. court system is that all arrests take place with warrants or good determination that probable cause exists. The court believes that a law enforcement ranger is a government advocate and is also aggressive in pursuing the duties and responsibilities of the position. Therefore, they prefer arrest with a warrant. Remember, the new ranger is always cautioned to make sure he/she knows what the jurisdiction is in his/her park. For example, in the state of Utah, all national parks are under proprietary jurisdiction. In one of these parks, such as Zion National Park, the only arrests a ranger can make are for those violations which are federal offenses under federal law (Larry Van Slyke).

Warrantless arrests must occur within the park or in a fleeing situation. While in such pursuit, rangers may pursue a suspect anywhere in the United States, although hot pursuit must meet certain criteria and the ranger must have the authority to arrest for the offense. The criteria for *hot pursuit* are as follows:

1. The ranger must have the authority to arrest a suspect for the crime. This includes a proper law enforcement commission.

2. The flight of the suspect must be to avoid arrest.

3. The pursuit must begin promptly and be continuous. There should not be any detours. You may stop for food, sleep, and to seek help, or in other pursuit related matters (FLETC, 1992).

When arresting for a felony without a warrant, the ranger must have probable cause that the person committed the crime. A delay in the arrest will not affect the validity of the arrest. This delay may give the ranger time to establish probable cause. If you find the remains of a grizzly bear in the backcountry, and you have reasonable suspicion to believe that the bear was illegally killed by an armed hiker, you do not have to make an immediate arrest based upon mere suspicion. Take the time to investigate the situation. Look over the facts and circumstances. The individual has to walk out of the backcountry. You will have plenty of opportunity to arrest the suspect, if indeed he is the suspect, although the arrest must occur in the park, unless the individual is fleeing.

You must have probable cause to arrest for a felony violation if it was not committed in your presence. Without probable cause, your arrest may be deemed an illegal arrest. Be careful when acting upon mere suspicion. If you are arresting the person for killing a grizzly on the word of a third party, the third party must identify the individual. This third party must also be a reliable informant. In court, you may have to prove the reliability of the informant. When in doubt, obtain an arrest warrant.

When arresting with a warrant, permanent level one rangers have the authority to serve arrest warrants and summons for the enforcement of federal law, regulations, and assimilated laws. A warrant can be served outside the park, anywhere in the United States for a crime under federal law committed in the park. A ranger can also arrest on a warrant in the park for an offense committed elsewhere.

— **Real Life Situation** ——————————

An employee at the houseboat concession on Lake Roosevelt at Coulee Dam NRA was found to have a current arrest warrant by the local sheriff's office. The sheriff's office contacted me and informed me about the warrant. I arranged for the man to meet me at the ranger station. I said I would like to speak to him about an incident which occurred at the concession. This was not true; I called him to the ranger station to arrest him on an arrest warrant from the county.

The deception was used in order to prevent the man from being aided by his friends at the concession. It was agreed upon by the deputy and myself that this would cause the least disturbance. The man came to the ranger station, and I arrested him. The warrant was issued for assaulting an officer and damage to property in a barroom brawl.

The General Authorities Act of 1976 directs national park rangers to cooperate with state and local law enforcement officers. There may be written agreements which set forth methods of warrant issuance. Be aware of these agreements. See the general provisions in NPS-9, Section III, chapter 4, page 2. Also see section II, Chapter 5, page 5 for the guidelines for the development of written agreements with other law enforcement agencies. The agreement, according to NPS-9, contains what each agency is to give and what they will receive. No agreement shall exceed the limit of five years.

WARRANT REQUIREMENTS

Warrants can be issued upon complaint, accompanied by an affidavit which establishes probable cause that an offense has been committed. Upon the request of a U.S. attorney, a summons, instead of a warrant, can be issued for an individual.

A *summons* is a document which differs from a warrant in that it is served to a suspect who is commanded by the court to present him/herself at a stated time and place. The summons may be served by actually handing the paper to the individual being served or by leaving it at the person's dwelling in the hands of a person of legal age and intelligence (FLETC, 1992). If the person fails to appear, then a warrant will be issued by the court. A warrant commands that the person be seized.

The warrant must be signed by the magistrate and contain the accused's name, or if the name is not known, a description by which the suspect can be identified. The warrant contains the charge against the individual and commands that the person be arrested and brought before the nearest magistrate. The warrant is executed by the arrest of the person named. (Ferdico)

Arrest warrants and summons will be prepared by your U.S. attorney and or his/her staff. The U.S. Attorney will review the complaint and the probable cause affidavit and present the document to the magistrate. The warrant is issued by the magistrate. The complaint document lists the probable cause and the elements of the crime. It is prepared by the ranger and presented to the U.S. attorney. This complaint provides the background for the arrest warrant.

The arrest warrant does not have to be in the ranger's possession at the time of arrest. Warrants can be issued over the telephone or radio, although the suspect must be made aware of the fact that a warrant has been issued for that individual's arrest.

After the arrest, the warrant is returned to the issuing magistrate. If a particular magistrate signed the warrant, bring the suspect before that magistrate. If you do not do this, you will have to obtain another warrant from the magistrate who you brought the suspect before. If the warrant is not served by a ranger, then it must be delivered to the U.S. Federal Marshal or other authorized law enforcement officer for execution. (FLETC, 1992)

The case, *Payton v. New York*, set forth precedent that law enforcement officers cannot make a warrantless arrest in a suspect's home for a felony. In addition, the seriousness of the offense is an important criteria. Although the seriousness of a crime is not enough to warrant a warrantless arrest in the suspect's home, warrantless arrests may be employed only to protect the house's occupants or to prevent the individuals' escape. There is no clear formula to plug all of the circumstances into. Rangers could prevent escape by surrounding the building and then wait for a warrant. Although if you are in hot pursuit of an individual, you do have exigent circumstances.

The case of *Steagold v. United States* states that you cannot go into the house of a third party to search for an offender without consent.

ARRESTS AND THE NCIC

Today, warrant information may be transmitted across the nation by computers. The FBI computers may be accessed by your local dispatcher upon your request. All rangers can detain or arrest individuals based upon the information received from this computer system. The information contained in this system concerns individuals wanted for specific offenses, stolen vehicles, stolen property, registered owners of vehicles, criminal histories of individuals, and drivers license information. If a person is listed as being wanted under an arrest warrant by the computer, then the person can be detained and arrested by the ranger. Extreme care must be used in this process, however. The information received by way of the computer must be verified before an arrest is made. Have your dispatcher call the issuing agency to verify the warrant (NPS-9).

AFTER THE ARREST

Take the arrested individual to the federal magistrate without any unnecessary delay. In the backcountry, delay may be necessary, due to extreme terrain, distance, or weather conditions. Unnecessary delay will not be tolerated by the magistrate. This is a fact. The only time a suspect will be held prior to the individual's initial appearance before the magistrate is over the weekend when the magistrate may be unavailable. In this circumstance, contact the U.S. Attorney's office for direction. In the jurisdiction of Coulee Dam NRA, the U.S. Attorney's office must be contacted prior to any arrest made in the park. They notify the magistrate and the Federal Marshal's office. The Federal Marshal's office must be notified because they will be responsible for safeguarding the individual while in a jail facility or in the federal courthouse. Seasonal rangers can assist in serving a warrant as long as they are with a full-time commissioned level-one ranger.

Travel time may dictate delay (i.e., delay may be deemed necessary when the magistrate is far away from the arrest site). The arrest procedure may also cause necessary delay. The procedure may include: background checks, warrant checks, finger-printing and photographing, treatment of a suspect's injuries or sickness, and voluntary confessions. A situation in which a suspect is confessing voluntarily is not considered to be an unnecessary delay. A confession during a period of unnecessary delay is not acceptable or admissible in court (NPS 9,1989). A ranger cannot pull over to the side of the road and coerce a confession out of an individual. This could involve just letting an individual sit handcuffed to a tree until the person confessed. A delay which is reasonable is allowed, but make every effort to document its reasonableness.

There are other post arrest obligations on the part of the ranger. They are as follows:

1. The ranger has a responsibility to care for a person in custody, medically or otherwise.

2. The ranger must provide protection for the prisoner from other prisoners.

3. The ranger must safeguard the property of the prisoner.

4. The person the ranger arrested must be housed in federally approved facilities.

5. Juvenile prisoners cannot be housed with adults. Make sure their parents or guardians are contacted.

6. Be aware that certain individuals are immune from arrest (e.g., diplomatic immunity) (NPS-9).

DIPLOMATIC IMMUNITY

Foreign diplomats and consular officers have diplomatic immunity. These individuals shall be accorded respective privileges, such as freedom from being forced to follow our laws. This immunity is granted according to the Vienna Convention on Consular Relations. This immunity can also be waived by the sending nation (NPS-9).

There are three different types of immunity:

1. Diplomatic agents and their families have full immunity.

2. The technical staff of the diplomat and their families also have full immunity.

3. The diplomat's service staff only have full immunity while at work, their families do not have immunity (FLETC, 1992).

Rangers are required to treat consular officers, consul-generals, and deputy consul-generals with due respect; they are entitled to limited immunity. They can only be arrested for grave crimes, such as felony arrests that would endanger the public. Even then these cases would be subject to court determination.

If a ranger stops a diplomat for a traffic violation, that does not constitute an arrest or a detention in the sense we referred to previously. The issuance of traffic citations does not constitute an arrest (NPS 9, 1989).

If a ranger arrests a person for driving while intoxicated, and that person turns out to be a diplomat, the ranger should call a taxi for the person or transport the diplomat home him/herself. Only restrain such a person if their own safety would be threatened. Even in a serious auto accident in which a diplomat is involved, there is a reporting sequence to follow. See the NPS-9 for further information.

ELEMENTS OF AN ARREST

There are four elements of arrest:

1. The intent a ranger has to arrest

2. The actual seizure of an individual

3. The ranger must communicate the intent to arrest to the person being arrested

4. The individual understands that he or she is under arrest (FLETC, 1992)

The intent to arrest means that the ranger must have the mental thought to take an individual into custody. This intent must be followed by the seizure or actual laying hands upon the person, or employing the use of a weapon. This could mean the display of a baton or firearm. It could include constructive seizure or peaceful arrest. The officer must communicate his/her intention to arrest. A ranger must tell the person that he/she is under arrest. The circumstances may warrant that this be communicated by the behavior of the ranger. For example, if the ranger arrests a person with a hearing disability. The ranger can use hand signs and display handcuffs to communicate with the arrested individual. Finally, the person must understand that the ranger intends to arrest him/her. The ranger's words and or actions communicate this to the individual. A ranger must know the elements of an arrest in order to understand at what point the person must be made aware of his/her *Miranda* rights. It is also necessary to know these elements in order to understand when an escape takes place. A person who does not understand that he/she is under arrest is not escaping when he/she walks away from a ranger. The full understanding of these elements makes a ranger aware of when he/she can search a person legally incident to an arrest.

LEVELS OF FORCE

Only the amount of force necessary to actuate an arrest may be used. Unnecessary force will not and can not be tolerated. One only has to think about the Rodney King incident in California to realize that force is only necessary when met with the same amount of resistance.

There are two types of force—deadly force and nonlethal force. *Deadly force* is force intended or likely to cause death or great bodily injury (NPS-9). This would include severe beatings and the use of some objects, such as handcuffs, batons, and firearms, depending upon the manner in which they were employed.

Deadly force should be employed when such force is necessary to overcome like force. A ranger must take the following into consideration:

1.   The nature of the offense. Are firearms or other deadly weapons involved in the situation?

2.   The behavior of the suspect. For example, a suspect is stopped in a vehicle, and the person reaches for a weapon which is laying on the seat. If you use deadly force be sure that you can articulate the dangerous behavior of the person. You must show that the circumstances caused you to fear for your safety or the safety of another.

3.   The actions of a third party may demand the use of deadly force. Other people may be present at the scene and decide to become involved on the suspect's behalf. For example, a ranger may approach what appears to be an innocent group of fishermen along a stream. The first person that is contacted may refuse to present a valid fishing license. A confrontation

arises between the ranger and the fisherman. The fisherman is joined by his comrades and the ranger is attacked en masse by knife-wielding fishermen. This is a situation for the use of deadly force. Consider the odds against the ranger. Four or five against one. A firearm may be the ranger's only alternative.

What are the alternatives to using deadly force? The ranger could try to talk his way out of the situation. Once away from a group, the ranger could call for backup and arrest the whole group without the use of deadly force. Remember, when there is a choice to leave or use deadly force, it is wise to leave and wait for help.

A ranger is justified in using deadly force to prevent his/her serious injury or death or that of another person. NPS-9 Section II Chapter 3, page 5 states that a ranger should never remove a weapon from the holster unless the potential for use exists. A ranger should never fire warning shots or use his/her weapon for the apprehension of a misdemeanor violation. A ranger must never use a weapon to fire at a moving vehicle unless the operator or occupant is attempting to use deadly force against the ranger or another person. The ranger is also prohibited from using a firearm as a striking weapon or to carry a firearm in a cocked position. The ranger violating any of these stipulations will be given the opportunity to explain the violation before a board of review.

Nonlethal force is defined by NPS-9 as, "Force not likely to cause death or serious bodily harm." Nonlethal force may be used to disperse unlawful groups, for self defense or in the defense of others. Examples of nonlethal force are chemical agents, such as pepper spray or mace, and a ranger's fists, forearms or feet.

A ranger must always avoid the application of a chemical agent directly to the face of a suspect. Never hit a suspect directly on the head with a baton or fist or other hard objects, such as a flashlight. A ranger must also remember to never use a chemical agent near an infant. After the suspect has been arrested, a restraining device should be used. All arrested persons must be placed in handcuffs. This will ensure the safety of the ranger and of the suspect, as well as the general public. The most important fact to remember is that no force may be used in an arrest unless that force is necessary, and then only the degree of force that is necessary may be used.

THE USE OF FORCE TO GAIN ENTRY

In some instances, rangers may use force to gain entry if they are refused entrance. This type of entrance may be necessary in cases where a search warrant is to be implemented and when there is a danger that the suspects may destroy evidence. In most cases, where warrants are served, rangers must announce themselves. Announcements are excused if the suspects may escape, the ranger's personal safety would be jeopardized, instances in which evidence might be destroyed, or the safety of other occupants may be imperiled. In addition to the above, "no-knock" warrants do not require announcements on the part of the rangers. In other situations, if you do not announce your presence, then you must document that fact.

MIRANDA

Prior to the Supreme Court's decision in *Miranda v. Arizona* (384 U.S. 436, 16 L.Ed. 2d 694, 86 S.Ct. 1602 (1966), a confession was admissible only if it was given voluntarily. Involuntary confessions violated due process, even if the confession was reliable. Before *Miranda*, voluntariness was established by the totality of circumstances surrounding the confession. (Lewis et al., 1973) This test was established by *Brown v. Mississippi* (1936), in which the Supreme Court held that a confession coerced from a defendant by means of police brutality violated due process of law. Later cases established other forms of police coercion which were prohibited, such as psychological abuse which could produce a coerced confession from a suspect. Other conduct also constituted a violation of due process, such as threats of violence, confinement of a suspect, deprivation of food or sleep, extended periods of interrogation, promises of leniency or trickery. The Court also examined the characteristics of a suspect and considered age, mental capacity, educational levels, physical or mental impairments, intoxication and prior experience with law enforcement.

Determination of the voluntariness of a confession or a totality of circumstances test can be summarized as follows: if the police did not use any coercion, then the statement would be considered voluntary. If the police used coercion, then the admissibility of the confession will be based upon the totality of the circumstances surrounding the giving of the statement, all other circumstances will be evaluated by the court.

In 1964, a major change took place with the case of *Escobedo v. Illinois.* The significance of *Escobedo* is that (1) it shifted inquiry from due process to the sixth amendment, and (2) the case did not follow the totality of circumstances approach. The Court took a single circumstance and made it the only factor in all cases in which it occurred. The Court said that when a process changes from investigatory to accusatory, and its purpose is to obtain a confession, then the accused must be allowed to consult an attorney. This opened the door for *Miranda.*

Miranda v. Arizona was decided two years later in 1966. In *Miranda v. Arizona,* the defendant was arrested in his home for rape and he was taken to the police station where he was identified by the victim. He was interrogated and signed a confession two hours later. At no time was *Miranda* advised of his right to consult an attorney, his right to have an attorney present during interrogation, or his right not to have to incriminate himself.

In *Miranda*, the court reviewed the facts and then discussed police interrogation techniques as prescribed in police training manuals. The Court said that the police then persuaded, tricked, or cajoled him out of exercising his constitutional rights. The Court then established procedural safeguards to protect the privilege against self-incrimination. These safeguards are as follows:

1) A suspect who is taken into custody and is subject to questioning must be warned of his rights prior to questioning.

2) The person must be told that s/he has the right to remain silent; that anything s/he says can be used against him/her in a court of law; that s/he has a right to an attorney, and if s/he cannot afford one, the court will appoint one. After these warnings have been given, the suspect can be told that s/he can waive these rights. The warnings must be given before the police question a person who is in custody or deprived him/her of freedom in any way.

There are exceptions to *Miranda*. One exception is a volunteered statement. Volunteered statements occur when a person walks up to a ranger and makes an incriminating statement, such as, "I just shot a grizzly bear." A ranger need not interpret a volunteered statement in order to warn a suspect of his/her *Miranda* rights. The *Miranda* decision states that rights need not be read if a person volunteers information freely.

Another exception are questions related to the public's safety. In *New York v. Quarles*, two officers were approached by a woman, who told them that she had been raped, and the man fled into a supermarket. One of the officers entered the store and observed the suspect who matched the description given by the woman. The officer arrested the man and asked him where the gun was after he discovered an empty shoulder holster. The man indicated that it was behind some boxes, and the officer recovered the weapon. The Supreme Court ruled that this was a public safety exception to the requirement that *Miranda* warnings be given before a suspect's answers may be admitted into evidence. In this situation, the Court used a balancing argument. The safety of society outweighed the need for protecting a suspect's Fifth Amendment rights against self-incrimination.

The *Miranda* warnings apply only to custodial interrogation conducted by law enforcement officers. Incriminating statements made by a person to a private citizen may also be inadmissible in court. In *Massiah v. United States*, after a defendant was indicted, federal agents obtained incriminating statements from Massiah in the absence of his attorney. While the defendant was free on bail, his codefendant interrogated him. These statements obtained from him were given to a government agent. Massiah was free to leave at any time, and he was unaware of any police dominated atmosphere, he was deceived (Cohen). The Court held that the statements were inadmissible because the defendant was denied the basic protection of his Sixth Amendment right to counsel.

In *Pennsylvania v. Muniz*, videotapes were introduced in court showing a person suspected of operating a motor vehicle under the influence of alcohol. The suspect had not been informed of his rights before the taping of his condition.

— Real Life Situation —————————————

On November 30, 1986, Officer David Spotts of the Upper Allen Pennsylvania Police Department noticed Inocenio Muniz stopped on the shoulder of the road. Officer Spotts observed Muniz and a passenger in the vehicle. The officer stopped Muniz, smelled alcohol on him, and noticed his bloodshot eyes and flushed face. Officer Spotts told Muniz to stay parked until he sobered up. Muniz assured the officer that he would. Muniz then pulled back on the highway and drove past Spotts. The officer stopped Muniz and gave him three sobriety tests, then he placed Muniz under arrest. Muniz was not given a *Miranda* warning at this time. Enroute to the station, Muniz offered statements concerning his drunkenness. He was booked at the station. At the booking he was videotaped, which was standard procedure, he was also asked various questions. He was given more sobriety tests while being taped. Before the third stage of videotaping, the Pennsylvania Implied Consent Law was explained to Muniz by a department employee. This law required that his permission be obtained to permit administration of a breath test to measure his blood alcohol level. He refused to take the test unless he could wait a couple of hours or have a drink of water. He was then read his *Miranda* rights.

Muniz was convicted at a bench trial on May 27, 1987. He appealed on the basis that the videotaping violated his right to be free from self-incrimination. The Court held that the slurred nature of speech and the related indicia of muscular coordination constituted physical evidence, and it lay outside the scope of *Miranda* protection.

In *Muniz,* the Court engaged in a balancing argument. The rights of an individual were weighed against the needs of society to be free from drunk drivers, and society won. The Court said that to be protected by the privilege against compelled self-incrimination, evidence must be a product of custodial interrogation, either express or implicit, and it must not be the product of routine booking questions. In this case, videotaping constituted physical evidence not testimonial evidence. This lays outside the scope of *Miranda.*

Booking questions are accepted as another exception to *Miranda.* There are others. In the inevitable discovery exception put forth by *Nix v. Williams,* the Court said that the evidence, in this case the body of a ten-year-old girl, would have been discovered anyway; therefore, it said that the evidence obtained because of an illegal confession was admissible. *Miranda* does not handcuff rangers; it provides protection, for both the ranger and the suspect.

Miranda does not always have to be given to a suspect. If a ranger requests a suspect to come to the station for questioning, and the person agrees, no *Miranda* warnings need to be given as long as the person is free to leave. In this manner, the ranger can question the person and any statement he/she receives can be used as evidence at trial. The ranger can then arrest the person after they have exited the ranger station.

When reading the *Miranda* warning, do not act upset or concerned. Relax and make sure that the suspect understands his/her rights. If you do not act upset, then the person may waive his/her rights and speak with you. There is no sense in messing up a good case. I suggest that rangers make use of summons and complaint citations instead of making arrests. If people are free until their court appearance, they can be more reasonable and compliant.

Remember that a waiver of a person's *Miranda* rights is not valid if deceit was used by the ranger. If a suspect does not understand his/her rights, read them to him/her again. If the person still doesn't understand his/her rights, do not question him/her. After a waiver is given, interrogation can begin. It must be stopped if the defendant asks for a lawyer. If you do not stop, then all the information which you have received up to that point could be jeopardized. Interrogation must stop when the suspect requests it to stop.

The Court states that you can resume the interrogation if the suspect wishes to talk, but you cannot question the suspect on the same material as before. You may only question the suspect if he asks to talk with you again.

The requirements of a second interrogation are as follows:

1. The first interrogation must have been terminated promptly.

2. A significant period of time must have passed.

3. The suspect must be given his full and complete *Miranda* rights again.

4. A different ranger resumes the interrogation.

5. The interrogation is restricted to a crime not the subject of the first interrogation (Ferdico).

Once a person is charged by the U.S. attorney's office all attempts to question a suspect should be stopped. If a person is to be released after an arrest, the release will only be done upon the request of the U.S. attorney; otherwise you cannot release the person. This release may be for any reason, even reasons not known to you. This is called *prosecutorial discretion*. The person can also be released by the magistrate or when the suspect meets the bail which has been set in court.

STOP AND FRISK

This type of stop will be discussed again in future chapters, but it should be briefly addressed here. The stop and frisk is a protection which a ranger offers him/herself. It is done to check a suspect for concealed weapons which are potentially dangerous to the ranger. The ranger should first have a reasonable suspicion that some criminal activity is taking place. In addition, the stop of the suspect must be a limited detention. If the stop is too long, it will become an arrest. It is an arrest if a reasonable person believes that they are not free to leave. The stop and frisk must be independently justified by articulating a reasonable fear of danger (Ferdico). For example, one night I received a call from my dispatcher that there was a report of a gang of youths harassing campers in the park. It was dark, and the report mentioned the possibility of firearms. I stopped and frisked the individuals I encountered in that area that evening, I was able to articulate a reasonable fear of danger because there were reported firearms nearby. The frisk must be limited to a search for weapons or items that could be weapons.

In order to avoid a contact with a visitor turning into a stop, be extremely polite; identify yourself as a ranger; do not demand anything from the visitor; explain why you are questioning the person; tell them they are free to leave; do not read them their *Miranda* rights; use no force; and do not frisk the person.

RESPONSIBILITIES OF AN ARRESTING RANGER

Arrest techniques may vary, but the fundamental responsibilities of the arresting officer do not change. The ranger has a number of responsibilities to consider. Self-preservation should be the first priority for the ranger. Do not take anything for granted. Do not relax your surveillance of the suspect. If the suspect makes requests following the arrest, all of these requests should be weighed very carefully. If granted they should be supervised very closely.

All suspects should be thoroughly searched at the time of the arrest, and at the time of transport, as well as at the time of booking. A suspect should not be permitted to speak with bystanders, as he/she may attempt to incite the crowd against you. You should remove the suspect from the scene as quickly as possible.

Bystanders are of major concern to the ranger. Their safety must always be considered during the arrest of an individual. If the arrest poses a possibility that an innocent person could be harmed, then the arrest should be postponed. This should always be taken into consideration when trying to stop a motorist in a high speed chase when in the frontcountry.

Finally, the ranger has responsibility for the person being arrested. The ranger must do everything he or she can to communicate the idea that the person is under arrest. It is good policy for the ranger to announce, "National Park Service ranger, you are under arrest." You must inform the suspect of the charges against him/her and notify the suspect about his rights under the Fifth and Sixth Amendments. Remember that all prisoners will be handcuffed, but care should be used to ensure that no injury results from the use of the cuffs.

There is no such thing as a routine arrest. They are all different. A lax ranger is a hazard to him/herself as well as to the public and the person being arrested. Be vigilant at all times. The use of deadly force should be avoided, if at all possible, and warning shots should never be used as per NPS-9. Make arrests if they are necessary, but use common sense in all your actions.

References

Cohen, Fred, "Miranda and Police Deception in Interrogation: A Comment on *Illinois v. Perkins.*" *Criminal Law Bulletin.* Nov./Dec. 1990. pp 534 - 546.

Epstein, Lee and Thomas Walker, *Constitutional Law for a Changing America.* (Washington D.C.: CQ Press) 1992, p. 393.

Ferdico, John N., *Criminal Procedure.* (St. Paul, MN: West Publishing Co.) 1989.

Federal Law Enforcement Training Center, *Training Guide.* (Washington D.C.: GPO) 1992.

Federal Criminal Code and Rules (St. Paul, MN: West Publishing Co.) 1988.

International Association of Police, *The Training Key* (Washington D.C.: Int. Assoc. of Police) 1965.

La Boeuf, Jacques, "5th Amendment - Videotaping Drunk Drivers: Limitations on Miranda's Protection." T*he Journal of Criminal Law and Criminology.* vol 81. no. 4. 1990, pp 883 - 925.

Lewis, Peter and Kenneth D. Peoples, *Constitutional Rights of the Accused* (Philadelphia: W.B. Saunders Co.) 1979, p. 444.

Walker, Samuel, S*ensation and Nonsense About Crime: A Policy Guide,* 2nd ed. (Pacific Grove, CA: Brooks/Cole Publishing Co.) 1989, p. 123.

CHAPTER 6

COURTROOM TESTIMONY

T his chapter examines the role of the U.S. magistrate in the federal court system. Proper courtroom demeanor and testifying techniques are discussed in addition to the functions of the U.S. attorney's office.

SUPREME COURT

When discussing the federal court system, it seems that the appropriate place to start is at the top with the Supreme Court. The Supreme Court reviews cases in order to determine the constitutionality of the case or law that is held in question. The Supreme Court does not utilize a jury, instead it consists of nine Supreme Court Justices who are appointed to life terms by the president. Cases heard by the Supreme Court are cases which are decided upon by at least four justices. Hundreds of cases are referred to the Court; however only very few are heard by the Court.

COURT OF APPEALS

The Court of Appeals is also a Federal Court of Review. This court is made up of three to five justices. Like the Supreme Court, they do not utilize a jury. The Court of Appeals reviews the decisions of the U.S. District Court. An appeal can be made if an error was made during any of the trial proceedings. The decision of the Court of Appeals can be reviewed by the U.S. Supreme Court. In fact, the U.S. Supreme Court must review all criminal appeals made to the Court of Appeals. They decide if the Court of Appeals acted properly or improperly.

U.S. DISTRICT COURT

The U.S. District Court hears cases at the trial level. Juries are utilized and the trials before U.S. magistrates can be appealed to the U.S. District Court. Federal justices who sit on U.S. District Courts are appointed for life, as are Appellate and Supreme Court justices. Federal magistrates are appointed by U.S. District Court justices.

Federal magistrates serve for terms of eight years. If the workload of a federal magistrate is not enough to warrant a full time magistrate then the district court justice can appoint a part-time magistrate, whose term is four years. Magistrates usually only work in the district in which they have been appointed. In order to be appointed, the person must be in good standing with the bar in the state which is part of that district. Citizens who are not attorneys may serve as part-time magistrates if the court is unable to appoint a qualified member of the bar at a specified location (FLETC, 1990).

In all likelihood, the magistrate will be the first officer of the court who a ranger comes in contact with. The magistrate is the judge that an arrested person is brought before for the initial appearance. The U.S. magistrate has the power to hear trials involving misdemeanors under Title 18 USC 3401, although a person may request that a district court judge hear his/her case.

The U.S. magistrate system was initiated to speed up the docket load of the district court. They can, and usually do, sign search and arrest warrants. They can handle all trials for misdemeanors including trials by jury, they can also sentence those convicted of a misdemeanor.

HOW A CASE COMES TO TRIAL

Rangers present their investigations to the U.S. attorney's office. The U.S. attorney may turn the report over to the grand jury for inquiry. The grand jury may also start an inquiry of their own. If the defendant in the case is not in custody at the time of indictment, the magistrate can issue an arrest warrant or a summons for their appearance in court. There are four ways to start a criminal proceeding before a magistrate:

1. A warrantless arrest made by a ranger for a crime committed in the ranger's presence or with probable cause.

2. The ranger can arrest with a warrant.

3. The grand jury can indict an individual.

4. The U.S. attorney can issue an information. This is basically a complaint filed with the magistrate, including probable cause.

Complaints are sworn statements by law enforcement rangers which contain specific facts constituting the offenses being charged to the defendant. The ranger usually has the assistance of the U.S. attorney in drawing up the complaint. The next step includes the arrest and initial appearance.

THE INITIAL APPEARANCE

During the initial appearance before a magistrate, the defendant is made aware of his/her constitutional rights. During the initial appearance, the magistrate informs the defendant of the following:

1. The charge and the maximum penalty

2. The defendant's right to retain counsel

3. For cases which are petty offenses, there is no right to counsel, otherwise the magistrate will offer to appoint a counsel if the defendant cannot afford one

4. The right to trial, judgement and sentencing before a U.S. district judge

5. The right to a trial by jury before a magistrate except for petty offenses

6. The right to a preliminary examination unless the defendant agrees to be tried before a magistrate.

7. If the defendant is in custody, the magistrate will inform the person about bail and how to secure pretrial release depending upon the circumstances.

If the person decides to accept trial before a magistrate, then the defendant signs a written consent to be tried before the magistrate; this waives the right to be tried before a U.S. District Court Judge. (Title 18 USC sec. 3401)

The initial appearance must take place as soon as possible. In a matter of hours, not days, or as soon as the next court is in session. However, it could be days if an arrest is made on a Friday night and the next session is Monday morning. Most arrests in our national parks occur on the weekends. The defendants usually end up spending their weekend behind bars.

THE PRELIMINARY EXAMINATION

This proceeding, sometimes called an Omnibus Hearing, determines if the arrest was proper. It determines if enough probable cause existed for the arrest. In this phase of the trial, the ranger gives testimony before the magistrate by way of questioning by the U.S. Attorney as to whether probable cause existed to make the arrest. An arraignment is conducted after probable cause has been established.

THE ARRAIGNMENT

The arraignment is the answer to a defendant's Sixth Amendment rights—the accused shall know the charges against him. The arraignment is conducted before the magistrate in open court. The arraignment consists of:

1. Calling the defendant forward

2. Reading the indictment or information to the defendant

3. The court will demand that the defendant enter a plea. The plea will be received by the court. Before the court will receive a plea the magistrate must be satisfied that the defendant has met with counsel and understands the plea.

Under Rule 11 of Title 18 USC 3401, a defendant may enter a plea of not guilty, guilty, or *nolo contendere*. If the defendant refuses to enter a plea, the magistrate will enter a plea of not guilty for the defendant. The court will accept a plea of guilty if the court determines that there is factual basis for this plea and that the plea was made voluntarily with the full understanding of the consequences. The plea of not guilty is a denial of the charge. This plea requires that the government prove the defendants guilt beyond a reasonable doubt. It carries with it the fullest protection of the defendant's constitutional rights. *Nolo contendere* does not contest the facts as charged, and for the purposes of punishment, it is the same as a guilty plea. It is not an admission of guilt, and because it is not, it cannot be used against a defendant as an admission in subsequent criminal or civil cases.

The U.S. attorney and the defendant's attorney may plea bargain according to Rule 11 (Federal Rules of Criminal Procedure). In exchange for a plea of guilty or *nolo contendere*, the government may agree to a lesser charge, recommend a dismissal of certain charges, or not contest the defense attorney's request for a specific sentence. Judges are not bound by such agreements. They also permit defendants to change their pleas if plea agreements are not accepted. In addition, defendants may change their pleas anytime before sentencing.

A BILL OF PARTICULARS

If the defendant asks for a Bill of Particulars, the person will be given a more detailed list of the charges against them.

THE DISCOVERY

The defense may request and see any portion of the government's case against the defendant prior to the trial. The Court may order the defendant the permission to inspect or photograph any of the following items:

1.   Statements of the defendant

2.   The prior criminal record of the defendant

3.   Documents, reports of examinations and tangible objects which are intended to be used as evidence and are necessary to the preparation of the defendants defense (Rule 16, Federal Rules of Criminal Procedure)

THE BRADY DOCTRINE

(BRADY V. MARYLAND, *373 U.S.83, 83 S.CT. 1194 1963*)

This Supreme Court decision gave the criminal defendant the discovery right of obtaining exculpatory evidence. The defendant is entitled to know what evidence the U.S. attorney holds that proves his/her guilt. The defendant is also entitled to any information that the government has showing the defendant's innocence. (For example, the government has information that the defendant was in the next county at the time of the commission of the crime.) The government has to provide this information only upon request. Motions are also made during the discovery process. These are known as pretrial motions. They may be written or oral depending upon the magistrate. For example, a motion to suppress is the process to exclude the use of evidence. There may be motions for the return of property, to dismiss the charges, and other motions which are heard in the judge's chambers (Federal Rules of Criminal Procedure, 1988).

THE TRIAL

The trial consists of four parts: jury selection, opening statements, evidence, and closing arguments.

The Constitution requires that the trial of crimes be held in the jurisdiction in which the crime was committed. This is known as *venue* (Fed R. Crim. p18, 1988). Therefore, venue is the particular district where a court may hear a case.

The functions of the judge and jury must also be understood in order to understand what a trial is. The judge decides the questions of law; presides over the court, directs the proceedings; conducts voir dire examinations of the jury, which simply are questions to determine if a juror meets the requirements to serve on the jury; instructs the jury; receives the verdict of the jury; and pronounces sentence.

The jury decides the questions of fact; however, a defendant may waive trial by jury and allow the judge to decide both question of law and of fact. The jury is selected from a panel of potential jurors. Twelve people are selected. There can be exceptions to this rule if both the defense and prosecution agree to a smaller number of jurors. The court may also direct that up to six alternate jurors be chosen. The alternates will sit through the entire trial, and then they will be excused after the jury has heard all of the arguments and is sequestered. The jury verdict must be unanimous in a federal criminal trial. The jury may find a person guilty of a lesser included offense but never of an offense more serious than the offense charged (Federal Rules of Criminal Procedure). For example, the jury may find a person guilty of larceny which is the lesser included offense in the charge of robbery.

The functions of the U.S. attorney are to guide and direct the government's case at the trial, to call the necessary government witnesses, to see that the evidence necessary to prove a case is presented, to conduct direct and redirect examinations of government witnesses, to cross-examine defense witnesses, and to see that all the necessary facts are brought before the court.

Direct examination is defined as the examination of a witness by the side who called the witness to the stand. A redirect examination is the reexamination of a witness after the opposition has cross-examined him or her. The attorney calling the witness has the right to reexamine a witness in order to explain answers given on cross-examination. The U.S. attorney's basic duty is to see that justice is accomplished.

The functions of the defense attorney are to conduct a defense of his client at trial, to guide and direct the defendant's case, to call defense witnesses, to cross-examine government witnesses, to conduct direct and redirect examinations of defense witnesses, and to make motions and objections on the behalf of the defendant.

The opening statements are directed to the jury by both the prosecuting attorney and the defense attorney. The prosecutor will address the jury first, and the defense attorney will address the jury second. The U.S. attorney will present any and all evidence to the jury first. This could be through the presentation of testimony, statements, documents, or tangible physical evidence, such as guns, bullets, and so forth. The foundation of submitting evidence is laid by questioning the ranger. For example, the attorney asks where the evidence was found or who made those statements. The accused doesn't have to testify because he/she is protected by the Fifth Amendment. Although once a defendant decides to testify, the defendant can be asked to incriminate himself. The defendant cannot choose to offer just favorable testimony. He/she must answer all of the prosecuting attorney's questions.

PRESENTATION OF EVIDENCE

The ranger has many hurdles to jump before evidence can be submitted in court. All evidence is subject to the Fourth Amendment. This was discussed in Chapter 2. It is also essential that the NPS-9 guidelines be followed in the obtaining of evidence and establishing its chain of custody. It is also necessary that rangers write clear, concise reports. If many arrests are made and reports filed, a ranger could confuse cases.

TRIAL CLOSURE

After both sides have presented all of their evidence, the attorneys can make their final closing arguments. They can argue their positions, in fact, they can say anything that they want to. The jury will make the final decision. The prosecuting attorney makes the first closing argument followed by the defense attorney. The U.S. attorney may also make a rebuttal argument, the defense attorney does not make a rebuttal to the rebuttal. If the jury brings a verdict of not guilty, the defendant goes free. If the jury finds the defendant guilty, there is another phase to the proceeding—the presentence investigation.

THE PRESENTENCE INVESTIGATION

The presentence report is prepared by the probation officer and is given to the magistrate as an aid in deciding on the proper sentence. It will contain information regarding the defendant's prior criminal record, his/her financial condition, personal characteristics and any other information relevant to the defendant's behavior. The judge sentences the defendant after being presented with the presentence investigation report.

THE SENTENCE

The judge will impose a sentence dependent upon the presentence investigation. In cases involving petty offenses, the sentence will be one consisting only of fines. In misdemeanor cases, the penalty may include fines, probation and/or jail time.

After the trial and sentencing, the convicted person has the right to appeal the decision. This right to appeal is only allowed in cases where the defendant has plead not guilty. The magistrate will advise the defendant regarding his/her appellate rights. There is no duty of the magistrate to advise an individual who has pled guilty or *nolo contendere* because there is no right to appeal in such an event.

TESTIFYING IN COURT

As a law enforcement backcountry ranger, you will be called to testify in court. It may be for a citation which you issued or an arrest which you made. It is an important aspect of being a backcountry ranger. As stated in the first chapter, you are a ranger because of people. You do not become a ranger to escape people, especially in the backcountry! It is important to present your testimony in the proper manner and with the proper demeanor.

The uniform you wear to court should be pressed and clean. Wear your dress uniform if at all possible. Remember, when testifying you are the center of the jury's or magistrate's attention. The courtroom is a place of dignity; your conduct and appearance should match your surroundings.

The ranger should be at the courthouse at a prearranged time, and notify the U.S. attorney's office of your arrival. Your testimony will be discussed and questions may be prearranged. It is also necessary to arrange testimony in sequence in order to build a case. If you can not arrive at the specified time, let the prosecutor know ahead of time because it is important to the building of the evidence.

When waiting to testify, do not talk about the case with fellow officers or other witnesses. The ranger may be confronted in cross-examination concerning statements the ranger made in the waiting area. Above all, do not discuss the case with unauthorized individuals. If you are asked by the defense attorney if you discussed this case with anyone, do not lie. Of course you have discussed this case with others—your supervisor, the U.S. attorney, family etc. Just answer truthfully.

When in the courtroom to testify, you should talk in a voice which everyone can hear. Hold up your hand in a manner befitting a National Park Service ranger, sit up straight in the witness chair and address the magistrate at a bench trial or the jury at a jury trial, when asked a question by either prosecutor or defense attorney. Make sure your testimony is heard by the jury, magistrate and court reporter. The ranger should show respect for the court and counsel by answering "yes sir" or "yes your honor," if addressing the judge or magistrate. Above all, never demonstrate your personal feelings when on the stand. When speaking, be objective.

Remember to use simple terms that can be easily understood by the jury or magistrate, avoid using police jargon. Never use sarcastic language when answering questions, especially upon cross-examination, and always reply with confidence.

After a ranger takes the stand, he/she will always be asked preliminary questions, such as name and position. When stating your name, always state your entire name and middle initial. The prosecutor will establish your credibility with these preliminary questions. They may also include questions about your background and your experience.

When it is time to leave the stand, you will be excused. Do not get up to leave before the magistrate is told that there are no further questions for the witness; the magistrate will excuse you. Do not display any emotion, such as relief or pleasure, just stand up and depart without saying another word.

The first thing to remember is to *always* tell the truth. Lawyers will always catch you in a story; they will tear it apart, and you will lose all of your credibility in the process. The U.S. attorney will do everything in his power to build your credibility. If you do not know the answer to a question, say, "I do not know." Don't make things up!

When you testify, you testify as to perceptions. These perceptions are gathered by your senses—seeing, hearing, smelling, and touching. Never state that a person was drunk, that is a conclusion. Always relate the statement to a perception: "The person smelled strongly of alcohol, and I heard him use slurred speech," or "I saw the person weave across the centerline of the road 15 times." Do not conclude that the person was intoxicated, merely relate to the magistrate or jury what you encountered through your senses. You can make conclusions after you become an expert in a particular field. Until that time, admit that you are not an expert. In order to establish your expertise, the foundation attributing to your expertise must be laid in court.

You cannot testify to what another person said. This is called *heresay*. There are exceptions, but they are beyond the scope of this chapter. Heresay is information related by another person to the witness. The heresay rule bars this type of testimony. An example of heresay testimony would be a case in which a backcountry ranger is investigating a bear poaching. The officer testifies that according to the statements of witnesses at the scene of the killing, Mr. Smith fired the shots which killed the grizzly. Obviously, since the investigating ranger did not see the bear get shot, he could not testify to his own personal knowledge of the incident. He merely related what someone else had seen. It would be necessary to put the eyewitness on the stand.

During your testimony, one side or the other may express an objection to the mode of questioning. Always pause for a brief period of time between answers to questions to allow for these objections. Give the attorneys time to make their objections. If they are improper, the objection will be overruled.

You will be examined directly by the prosecuting attorney. You will be asked open-ended questions, such as "What are your job duties?" Feel free to answer these questions in your own words. The U.S. attorney will have previewed these questions and answers with you prior to testifying. Do not throw your U.S. attorney a curve, answer in the prearranged manner.

In the cross-examination by the defense attorney, you may be asked some leading questions, such as whether on the night the grizzly was killed it was dark. Answer "yes" or "no"; you cannot qualify the statement. It was night, it had to have been dark. If you have enough faith in the prosecutor, then perhaps you could answer with a qualifying answer, "Yes, it was night, but the moon was full." The prosecutor could bring this out in a redirect examination.

The tactics of the defense attorney during the cross-examination are designed to cloud the testimony of the ranger, in other words, to cast doubt into the minds of the judge or jury. The defense attorney may rephrase questions and ask you them over and over again, trying to seek out different answers. The best defense to this is to know the facts and to listen carefully.

The defense attorney will always ask you if you read the defendant his rights. Always state that you read the people you arrest their rights the same way every time, right off of the card.

The defense attorney may try to ask complex questions which cannot be answered with a simple yes or no. The defense may sometimes demand a yes or no answer. You can appeal to the magistrate by explaining that you cannot answer the question with a simple yes or no.

Occasionally, the defense will resort to rapid fire questions. These are designed to make the witness answer with inconsistent statements. Remain calm, take your time and ask to have the question repeated. Be aware of certain trick questions, which are intended to attack your credibility. These may be questions as to whether or not you drink or gamble. If the truthful answer is yes, give it quickly and firmly. The ranger may be asked if he/she ever violated the law? Answer yes, if necessary, and qualify it. Who hasn't committed a minor traffic violation?

The defense attorney may try a various number of tactics to disqualify a ranger on the witness stand. You may be asked about your authority to arrest or carry firearms. Know where it comes from (i.e., the General Authorities Act of 1976). The defense may ask you hypothetical questions. This type of question is also designed to cast doubt into the mind of the jury or the magistrate. The defense may ask condescending questions to make the witness feel inferior. The defense may approach the witness in a friendly manner in order to mislead the witness and lull the witness into complacency so the witness will also lose credibility.

Badgering tactics may be employed in order to make the ranger angry. Such badgering will usually be met with an objection by the U.S. Attorney. The defense attorney may stare at you in a quizzical manner. This is done to confuse you and to get you to repeat your answer. Answer once, and if it is needed, the defense will ask you again; do not volunteer a second answer. The ranger should listen carefully to all questions and answer as concisely as possible. The defense counsel will try to discredit a ranger's testimony. If successful it may be next to impossible for the prosecutor to reestablish your credibility.

Another item of contention is usually time and distance. A defense attorney will usually try to pin an officer down as to the exact time or distance involved in a case. Be explicit in all of your reports and state that a distance or time was an approximation (e.g., the distance was approximately two miles). If you cannot remember the distance in court, say so. If it is a guess, say so. If possible do not make guesses, although the defense attorney may try to show that you are not cooperative if you do not guess. Just tell the magistrate or the jury that to guess would be total speculation on your part.

The defense attorney will probably cross-examine you based upon your report. The purpose of the report is to include all pertinent facts of the incident. If you state something different in your testimony than was in your report, the defense attorney may try to label you as a liar.

When testifying, if you make a mistake, own up to it. If you do this, then the U.S. attorney will trust you in the future. When you hear a question that confuses you, say so, and ask for clarification. You must also trust your U.S. attorney.

SUMMARY OF GUIDELINES WHEN TESTIFYING

- Good appearance
- Be prepared
- Be truthful
- Be calm and courteous
- Be objective, do not lose your temper
- Speak loudly and listen to the questions
- Take your time
- Do not guess
- Speak directly to the magistrate or jury
- Leave when excused

References

Federal Criminal Code and Rules (St. Paul, MN: West Publishing Co.) 1988.

Federal Law Enforcement Training Center, *Criminal Testimony Pamphlet* (Washington D.C. : Govt. Printing Office) 1992.

Ferdico, John N., *Criminal Procedure* (St. Paul, MN: West Publishing Co.) 1989.

U.S. Department of Justice, *Preparing to Testify* (Washington D.C.: Government Printing Office) 1984.

CHAPTER 7

RANGER ETHICS AND LIABILITY

E thics and liability appear to be a strange combination; however, I believe that they go hand in hand. The purpose of this section is to make either a potential or new ranger aware of the liability which may accrue, both personally and professionally, for actions or omissions while on duty. In order to avoid aspects of negative liability, a uniformed law enforcement ranger must establish and maintain a high ethical code when dealing with the general public. In addition, the ranger must understand his/her rights, responsibilities and duties to the public. Although, he/she may work in a relatively remote area, the ranger's actions are always under close scrutiny.

RANGER LIABILITY

Initially, liability suits against federal employees were generally rare, although they did occur periodically. In 1971, the Supreme Court held in *Bivens v. Six Unknown Federal Narcotics Agents*, 403 U.S. 388 (1971) that federal officers can be held responsible for offenses against the Fourth Amendment. The old doctrine of *official immunity* for law enforcement officers died with this case. *Bivens* established new criteria for violations of the Fourth Amendment. Because of this decision, only *qualified immunity* would be available to federal law enforcement officials.

Bivens v. Six Unknown Federal Narcotics Agents
403 U.S. 388 (1971)

In 1965, Federal Narcotic Agents entered Biven's home and searched it without a warrant. They used excessive force in arresting him and frightened his family. Ordinarily this case would have had to have been brought before a state court. In order to avoid this, Biven's attorney argued that these acts violated Biven's Constitutional rights, afforded by the Fourth Amendment. The Supreme Court ruled that such wrongdoing by federal agents should be adjudicated by a federal court. Because there was no federal remedy for this violation, the Supreme Court created one. Federal agents are now subject to civil suits for alleged Constitutional violations committed by them.

The Supreme Court has afforded individuals complaining of officer indiscretions the right to bring those individuals to court and require that they answer for those wrongdoings. Those consist of the following:

1. Illegal search and seizure

2. The use of excessive force

3. The commission of assault and battery by an officer

4. Officer coercion to obtain an admission

5. Malicious prosecution of a suspect

The Court hoped to protect the individual's rights to consult with an attorney, protect against self-incrimination, and receive prompt arraignment after an arrest. The Court does not require that an individual be informed as to the reason for his/her arrest; to be read *Miranda* rights, if he/she is not subject to direct questioning; or to be free from libel and slander from a ranger. These latter points would not be grounds for a liability suit against a ranger. I, however, do not recommend that rangers make it a policy to not inform a person of the charges against him/her or not read them their *Miranda* rights after arrest.

QUALIFIED IMMUNITY

Rangers are protected by immunity. At one time, the protection of absolute immunity was available to officers of the law. Today, there is no such thing as absolute immunity; federal law enforcement officers are protected from liability by qualified immunity. *Qualified immunity* is immunity from liability if the officer is performing his or her duties according to the requirements and guidelines established by law. In the past, officers were immune simply because they were officers of the federal government. This was called *absolute immunity*. Absolute immunity is simply immunity without qualification. No federal officer could be held liable for any actions if there was a guarantee of absolute immunity.

Qualified immunity is an affirmative defense in a liability suit. If proven, the burden of proof is on the officer; it is immunity from suit not just from liability. The Court ruled in 1982 "... an official's entitlement to qualified immunity is established if it is proved by objective standards that there is no violation of clearly established constitutional guarantees" (457 U.S. at 818). Qualified immunity is designed to protect federal officers from lawsuits and the need to go to trial. The Supreme Court has also held that denials of qualified immunity are immediately appealable (*Mitchell v. Forsyth*, 105 S. 2806, 2816 (1985).

LIABILITY AND THE GOVERNMENT

Just how many federal officers and officials are sued for liability issues? In 1986, according to Farley, there were nearly

3,000 suits pending against 10,000 officials. There were only 32 adverse decisions against those various officials. Who defends these officers and officials in court?

According to 28 USC 516-519, The U.S. attorney general and the justice department are responsible for representing employees of the United States government for suits against them while in performance of their duties for their country. The Department of Justice has also represented government employees who are personally sued for monetary damages because of actions undertaken in their official capacity.

There are two criteria which must be met in order to be defended by the justice department. The first is the scope of employment, and the second is the interest of the United States. The *scope of employment* means that the employee's actions must reasonably appear to have arisen because of the type of job the person had with the government. This employment includes individuals who are officers or employees of any federal agency, military personnel, and persons acting on the behalf of government agencies (FLETC, 1991).

"Interest of the United States" means that the representation of the person must be in the interest of our government. By representing employees, it encourages them to vigorously perform the duties mandated by their job (FLETC, 1991). For example, a ranger who fully knows and expects to be defended if he/she makes a mistake in arresting an individual for shooting a grizzly will not hesitate in vigorously pursuing the poacher. If the ranger has to worry constantly about liability suits, the ranger's performance could definitely suffer and the poacher could get away.

Representation by the justice department is neither compulsory nor automatic. A federal ranger can choose to hire his or her own attorney. The U.S. attorney chosen to defend an employee will be from the district where the litigation originated. The Department of Justice will not initiate suits on the behalf of employees that are not in the best interest of the United States. In the event of an adverse judgement, the employee is solely responsible for damages payable to the plaintiff; it is not the responsibility of the U.S. Government. In some cases governed by exceptional circumstances, the government might indemnify the employee and pay the damages.

A ranger will not be provided Department of Justice representation if he/she is charged with federal criminal proceedings or in agency investigations. Federal officers are not immune from criminal proceedings because of their employment status. However, they are immune from state criminal processes and proceedings because of the Supremacy Clause of the U.S. Constitution, which provides that the employee's actions are authorized by federal law.

When do law enforcement rangers place themselves in a position in which their actions or inactions cause them to accrue liability? One way is when the ranger is acting under the "color of law." *Color of law* is when a member of the public has a reasonable belief that the ranger has some authority due to the uniform the ranger is wearing or the equipment or vehicle the ranger may be using.

A ranger may incur personal liability for the use of excess force when making an arrest under the "color of law." A ranger may also be liable when he or she is at home or not on duty. For example, a ranger goes home and encounters and apprehends a burglar while still in uniform. The ranger is still acting under the color of law. Whenever rangers are in uniform, they are subject to civil liabilities, whether they are performing their duties or not. Remember that a civil action is not a criminal action. Title 42 USC 1983 addresses civil action. Title 18 USC 242 addresses criminal liability while a ranger is acting under the color of law.

A civil action against a ranger is not under the control of the U.S. attorney; only liabilities which fall into the category of criminal liability are handled by that office. Criminal liability carries criminal penalties. Civil liabilities carry civil penalties known as *damages*. These damage cases are tried in civil court and are known as *tort claims*. This is the manner in which the legislature provides an avenue for injured people to sue the government or its representatives. The burden of proof in a civil tort case is a preponderance of evidence. It doesn't have to be proven beyond a reasonable doubt as in a criminal case.

The Federal Tort Claims Act allows a citizen to sue the government in certain types of cases when the United States is named a party in the civil suit. This is an added protection for law enforcement rangers—it is good to have the United States as a partner in the lawsuit. The government will not be able to abandon you, their partner. If a ranger is sued, the trial is held in the jurisdiction in which the plaintiff resides. Therefore, a ranger could conceivably be drawn into lawsuits all around the country. After all, that's where the visitors come from. A last point to make about federal torts is that they do not exist. The federal government looks toward state law to determine what the tort or civil wrong is.

Some reasons rangers are sued under the Federal Tort Claims act are for false arrest, false imprisonment and excessive force. In the situation of false arrest, perhaps the ranger did not have adequate or *any* probable cause. If excessive force is used to make an arrest, this could be cause for a liability suit. This may include a death or severe bodily injury. If a person was killed in the process of being arrested, the family of that person might decide to sue the ranger because he or she used excessive force. All of these torts do not necessarily mean that the ranger made a mistake.

Rangers are also protected under good faith immunity. *Good faith immunity* assures rangers that they will be free from the fear of liability suits if they act as a reasonable individual within the scope of their employment or authority. This can be used as a defense in a civil suit against a ranger. For example, suppose you stop an individual with a rifle on the edge of your park's boundary, the rifle muzzle is still hot, and there is a deer carcass on the inside of the park. You arrest the individual for poaching. Subsequently, it is established that the individual didn't poach the deer, the deer was shot by another hunter and just happened to die in that location. The hunter you arrested, shot at and missed another animal outside of the boundary. The ranger arrested the suspect in good faith and would be able to use that as a defense in a liability suit.

NEGLIGENCE

The omission of an action may also be grounds for a liability suit against a ranger. This omission may be defined as *negligence*. In order to prove negligence, four criteria must be met:

1) The ranger must have a duty to conform to a specific standard of conduct in order to protect the visitor.

2) The ranger must have failed to conform to that standard.

3) That failure must be the proximate cause of the visitor's injury.

4) There must be damage or injury.

Other types of liability torts are related to invasion of privacy, abuse of process, cruel and inhuman punishment, and negligent vehicle operation. The invasion of privacy tort may involve an injury to an individual's character. If a person is arrested, the mere fact that they were arrested may blotch their character. If the sanctity of an individual's home is violated illegally, the person may be entitled to a damage settlement under this liability tort. The *abuse of process* involves the fraudulent use of a warrant to search for items beyond the scope of the warrant. Cruel and inhuman punishment could apply to rangers if they denied a prisoner medical aid. When it comes to negligent vehicle operation, the rangers are afforded no special privilege to break traffic laws. Some states have special emergency vehicle codes, but the officer is still expected to exercise reasonable care in the operation of an emergency vehicle. If a person is injured because of a mishap with an emergency vehicle, the court will determine if the ranger acted as a reasonable individual should act under those circumstances.

Civil Rights Protection

Title 18 USC 241

This is a criminal statute about conspiracy against the rights of citizens by two or more people. This law guarantees that if anyone hinders a person in enjoying or exercising any right given by the Constitution or the laws of the United States, those individuals will be fined not more than $10,000 or not imprisoned for less than ten years or both. If death is the direct result, the penalty shall be life imprisonment. (Federal Criminal Code and Rules, 1988)

Title 18 USC 242

This statute concerns the deprivation of a citizen's rights, privileges or immunities protected by the Constitution, under the color of law; it also concerns the administration of punishment, pain or penalty because of race, color or country of origin. The penalty for such violation shall be a fine of $1,000 and or imprisonment of not more than one year (Federal Criminal Code and Rules, 1988).

Title 18 USC 245

This statute states that there are certain protected federal activities in which all citizens may participate. Individuals acting under the color of law, by either threat or force, who willfully interfere with the following activities are to be held in violation of federal law. Those activities are as follows: voting; qualifying to vote; campaigning and or qualifying as a candidate for election; participating or exercising any right and or privilege as a citizen of the United States; applying or enjoying employment within any agency of the U.S. Government; serving as a juror; and participating in or receiving benefits from any federal financial program.

This statute applies to any person of race, color, religion, or national origin. This includes the enrollment in, or attendance of, public schools or public colleges; applying for employment; serving as a juror; traveling or using any public facility; enjoying the goods, services, accommodations of any hotel, motion picture house, sports arena, or any type of exhibition or public entertainment facility; and this statute affords all persons the right to be free from discrimination (Federal Criminal Code and Rules, 1988).

This statute is not meant to stop rangers from enforcing the laws, but to protect all people from the illegal enforcement of laws which may deprive certain individuals of their Constitutional rights.

The violator of this statute will be fined not more than $1,000 or imprisoned not more than one year, or both. If bodily injury results, the fine shall increase to $10,000. If death is the result, then the penalty will be imprisonment for up to life.

Title 42 USC 1983

This statute states that the violation of an individual's Constitutional rights by another acting under the color of law is a case that will afford a civil cause of action. The officer who commits such a wrong will be liable in civil court. Section 1983 only applies to state, county, and local officers, not to federal officers.

DAMAGES AND AWARDS FOR CLAIMS

The head of a federal agency may consider and settle any claim for money damages against the United States for injury or property loss caused by the negligence, action, or omission of any employee of the agency acting within the scope of his or her authority or employment, provided the settlement does not exceed $25,000 (FLETC, 1991 p.CLF-6). Any award more than this dollar amount must first be approved by the attorney general. The acceptance of this kind of settlement shall be final and will constitute a release of any claim against the government or the employee. If the United States denies the claim, then the person will have the right to file suit against the United States and its employee in U.S. District Court (FLETC, 1991).

STATUTE OF LIMITATIONS

A two year statute of limitation applies to all tort claims against the government of the United States (FLETC. 1991).

ETHICS

Backcountry law enforcement rangers are professional law enforcement officers. When professionals unite to form groups, they set down fundamental principles. These principles are used to guide them in common decision making. The primary factor which elevates "rangering" to the professional level is a code of conduct. When all rangers abide by this code, then "rangering" becomes a true profession. The *National Park Service Law Enforcement Code of Ethics* is as follows:

> I will faithfully abide by all laws, rules, regulations, and policies governing the performance of my duties and I will commit no act that violates these laws and regulations, or the spirit or intent of such laws and regulations while on or off duty.
>
> In my personal and official activities, I will never knowingly violate any local, state, or Federal laws and regulations, recognizing that I hold a unique position of public trust which carries an inherent personal commitment to uphold laws and the integrity of my profession. For these reasons, I understand that this code places special demands on me to preserve the confidence of the public, my peers, my supervisors, and society in general.
>
> I will commit no act in the conduct of official business or in my personal life that subjects the Depart-

ment of Interior and the National Park Service to public censure or adverse criticism.

While a commissioned employee, I will neither accept outside employment nor make any display representative of the Department or the National Park Service that will in any way conflict with the law enforcement interests or jeopardize the activities or mission of the Department of the Interior or the National park Service, or give the appearance of conflicts. I will also comply with the Departmental rules and regulations regarding employee conduct.

As a commissioned employee and representative of the Department of the Interior and the National Park Service, I will conduct all investigations and law enforcement functions assigned to me impartially and thoroughly, and report the results thereof fully, objectively, and with meticulous accuracy.

In investigative process, I will be judicious at all times and I will release information pertaining to my official duties, orally or in writing, only in accordance with the law and established policy.

In connection with my official duties, I will accept no gift, gratuity, entertainment or loan except as provided by Departmental regulations. I will not accept favored treatment of any kind, from anyone on my own behalf or on behalf of any other person, recognizing that acceptance may result in a conflict or give the appearance of conflict with my official duties or hinder my effectiveness as a commissioned ranger.

I will abide by all the rules, regulations, and policies of the Department and National Park Service including those relating to health, safety, and technical requirements of my position (NPS-9, 1989, p2-3, Chapter 5, Section I).

As a park ranger, you will always be under close scrutiny by the public. This will occur in your professional life and your personal life. The public will base their opinions of you and your agency on your conduct. Because of this, it is of the utmost importance that you conduct your activities according to the rules and regulations of the National Park Service.

In order to conduct yourself ethically, you must understand what ethics are. *Ethics* are a set of rules for conduct in specialized areas of expertise (Force, 1993). Ethical conduct is a combination of good judgement and common sense. For example, rangers should know not to drive into the backcountry on a closed fire road in the park and use his/her master key to gain access for personal enjoyment. Use common sense and good judgement before making any decision.

Many young potential rangers never become rangers because they failed to use good judgement and common sense. They commit what they consider minor indiscretions and are charged with a misdemeanor. The charge of poaching prior to applying for a position of ranger will surely be a consideration of the hiring supervisor. The young person with such a record will probably not be hired. Think about the consequences of illegal actions. Do not commit transgressions against the laws of our government. Use common sense and good judgement. A moral human value system is the foundation of a good backcountry ranger.

The code of ethics for all professional groups can fit in the category of an individual's relationship to society—the obedience of a member of society to society's rules and regulations. The utilitarian philosophy — the good of the many outweighs the good of the few — surely fits into this category.

The public forms its opinion of you from your current actions. The public does not base its opinion on your reputation. One bad act can ruin the efforts of an entire staff. If a violator uses foul language and you retort with foul language, that is unethical behavior. It is behavior that is not acceptable.

It is considered unethical to use your badge and credentials immorally or illegally. For example, if you keep your driver's license in the same case as your commission for the sole purpose of presenting it when you are stopped by another officer for a traffic violation, it is unethical behavior. The acceptance of gifts and bribes is definitely an unethical practice. Outside activity or employment which is not compatible with your scope of employment as a ranger is not ethical. To habitually use alcohol and other controlled substances is definitely unethical behavior for a law enforcement ranger. The misuse of government vehicles is not allowed and the private use of government vehicles is an ethical violation. These are just a few areas of ethical concern. If you observe a fellow employee violating certain standards of conduct, the necessary action is your responsibility. If you do not take the necessary action and someone else is seriously injured, then the fault may lie with you. Act responsibly, use good judgement and exercise common sense in all of your actions. This includes your off duty activities and habits as well as the time you spend on the job. My advice to all of you is to think honestly and morally. Remember to treat everyone with Respect, Honesty, Objectivity, Morality, and Prudence (i.e., RHOMP).

Backcountry rangers have an ethical responsibility to safeguard human life. They also have the same obligation to the land, water, plants, minerals, wildlife, and all other living things. Aldo Leopold's "Land Ethic" fits into this category. The backcountry ranger has a responsibility to preserve and protect the natural integrity of the backcountry. There is an ethical obligation and ecological necessity to respect the "land." This belief in ethics reflects a ranger's conviction towards a human and an ecological conscience.

References

Federal Criminal Code and Rules (Washington D.C.: Government Printing Office) 1988.

FLETC, *Student Guide to Ethics* (Washington D.C. : Government Printing Office) 1986.

FLETC, *Officer Liability* (Washington D.C.: Government Printing Office) 1991.

Force, Jo Ellen, Lecture notes from The University of Idaho, *Forest Policy*, 1993.

International Association of Police, "Professional Police Ethics," *The Training Key* (Washington D.C.: Int. Assoc. of Police) 1964.

Leopold, Aldo, *A Sand County Almanac*, Oxford University Press, 1949.

National Park Service, NPS-9 (Washington D.C.: Govt. Printing Office) 1989.

PART II

Part II contains the results of a year long study. Rangers were contacted in 29 national parks and questioned about various law enforcement problems that occur in their respective parks. These law enforcement problems ranged from minor resource violations, such as illegal campfires, camping in undesignated areas, camping without permits, pets off leash and damage to park vegetation; to major violations, such as poaching, drug cultivation and violent crimes. All of the examples of these problems are real life situations encountered by real national park rangers.

The following table lists the major violations which occurred in each of the 29 national parks in which interviews were conducted. The "X" indicates that this violation occurred within the park.

Park Name	Poaching	Off-Rd Travel	Drugs	ARPA	Violent Crime
Great Basin	X	X		X	X
Haleakala		X			
Everglades	X	X			
Craters / Moon	X				
Gr Smky Mts	X				
Lake Mead		X	X	X	X
N. Cascades		X			
Voyagers	X	X	X		
Acadia	X	X	X		X
Crater Lake	X				
Yellowstone	X				
Sequoia Kings Cyn	X			X	X
Glacier	X				X
Denali		X			
Big Bend		X	X		X
Wrangell St. Elias	X	X			
Zion			X		X
Glen Cyn			X		X
Isle Royale					
Whiskeytwn	X		X		X
Yosemite	X		X		X
Arches	X	X	X	X	
Shenandoah	X			X	X
T Roosevelt	X	X			
Cyn Lands		X		X	X
Bryce Cyn	X	X			
Olympic	X				
Grand Canyon		X	X	X	X
Death Vly	X	X	X	X	X
% Totals	66%	55%	38%	28%	48%

Serious park violations in 29 National Parks

CHAPTER 8

POACHING IN THE NATIONAL PARKS

T his portion of the text begins with a discussion of the most prevalent problem in the backcountry of our national parks—poaching.

Poaching is not a new problem in natural resource areas. Poaching is almost an institution in parts of the United States. In 66 percent of the 29 national parks in which interviews of rangers were conducted, rangers reported that poaching was a major violation. The poacher is regarded as a hero in some social circles, a person who only takes game in order to survive. Borrelli said, "The glorification of a poacher as a folk hero; a bold freebooter of the woods. . .like Robin Hood demonstrates the resilience of a frontier myth; a traditionally ingrained antagonism toward game laws and their enforcers." In this case, the enforcer is the National Park Service Law Enforcement ranger, not the Sheriff of Nottingham. The game that is being stolen does not belong to a rich nobleman, it belongs to all of the people of the United States. The places where this illegal activity occurs are the areas set aside for all generations to enjoy. Few, if any, poachers today take game just to survive. Many poachers illegally take game from our parks just to boast about. Some take trophy animals for the huge profits their parts will bring in the market places of the Far East. No matter the reason, the poachers must be identified, and their illegal activities must be halted.

PROFILE OF A POACHER

Poachers cannot be stereotyped. They are not all rough seasoned men of the woods. They are people seeking an easy way to make a "buck" who put their personal gain or convenience above the rights of society. The following is a profile of a game violator. This profile is a compilation of information from many natural resource law enforcement officers.

Poachers who operate in national parks and adjacent lands usually live within 25 miles of the park in question. Most of these individuals are in their 20s and 30s. These poachers usually hunt in groups or parties, both for waterfowl and deer. Nonprofit poachers may be members of sportsmen clubs or other hunter groups. They usually poach late into the winter season when there are fewer people in the parks and typically on Fridays and Saturdays. (This is especially true in parks such as Great Smoky Mountains National Park. This park experiences a lot of black bear poaching.) Poachers tend to be highly educated white collar workers, farmers or students. These individuals believe that the park regulations are unfair or not necessary. All of them are tempted by the abundance of trophy animals in our parks. Finally, the poacher finds it challenging and adventurous to outwit the law and the law enforcement ranger; sometimes they do it out of a sense of retribution and rationalize the crime. As one illegal hunter in the Great Basin National Park told a ranger," My family hunted here for generations before the Park Service moved in, I never intend to quit my hunting on this property."

POACHERS AND LAW ENFORCEMENT RANGERS

Violators do not perceive a risk of being apprehended by a bunch of "tree hugging cops." They do not perceive law enforcement rangers in the national parks as *real* law enforcement officers. This is illustrated by the summer visitors' shock at seeing rangers wear defensive equipment such as sidearms. The public does not tend to differentiate between law enforcement rangers and interpretive or general rangers. In parks, if hunters believed that rangers could and would catch them poaching, then poaching

During the hunting seasons around our national parks, the Park Service needs to increase their patrols and ranger force. Other methods to prevent poaching are being tried by various parks throughout the system.

PARKS, POACHING AND SOLUTIONS

Bruce Edmonston, Chief Ranger at Craters of the Moon National Monument, thinks poaching is a large problem in his park. He believes that a boundary fence may be one way to solve the problem. A fence would be a physical barrier which hunters would have to cross. If they cross the fence, then they cannot plead ignorance regarding the location of the park's boundary. Bruce also intends to erect large signs on the boundaries informing would be poachers that they are crossing the park's boundary.

He also stated that during the hunting season the rangers at the monument initiate a policy of heavy visitor contact. Bruce said, "We go after them wherever we find them, we give them a map and tell them about the boundary, we will do upwards of 200 contacts in the first week of the state hunting season." It seems that the poaching problem at Craters of the Moon is split between poachers who are there intentionally and hunters who do not have a clue as to where the boundary is. Edmonston states that, "There are some real illiterates out here, that hunt here. There is a fence, they don't read the sign, they're just kind of 'stupid.' The other ones know what they are doing."

Craters of the Moon National Monument has the only protected deer herd in the state of Idaho. They have trophy size animals in that herd. Rangers have contacted hunters who come from other states to hunt near the park because they have heard about this trophy herd of mule deer. If these hunters cross the boundary, the rangers automatically issue a citation and confiscate their weapons. They then escort them out of the park and send them on their way. Poachers who are caught in the park are sometimes prosecuted in federal court and in state court for their violations.

On the north boundary of the park, individuals walk the boundary, hoping for a shot at a trophy animal. Occasionally, the deer is too big and too close to the line to pass up. They shoot and cross the line. Most of the time they get away with it because the park is understaffed. Actually understaffing is a large part of the poaching problem. This also seems to be the situation in Wrangell St. Elias National Park and Preserve in Alaska.

— Real Life Situation —————————

A typical situation encountered at the park is the drive–through poaching incident. Many hunters search for game by driving the highways in the park. It is not legal, but they do it anyway. The hunters will drive through the park, see a deer cross the highway, stop along the shoulder of the road, jump out of their vehicle and start shooting at the deer.

One incident involved two different vehicles, the individuals didn't even know each other. They all jumped out of their vehicles, about three hundred yards from the visitor center, and started shooting. They got their deer, but the rangers got them.

Wildlife poaching is a serious problem in Wrangell St. Elias, says Chief Ranger Jay Wells. Although 18 big game guide operations operate legally within the preserve portion of the park, a commercial permit from the National Park Service is needed in order to do business there. This provision is often flagrantly violated.

Individuals take game out of season. They shoot trophies and fail to salvage the meat from the animal, and they commit Lacey Act violations when they illegally transport game out of the area. Renegade commercial outfitters work the park and preserve without commercial permits. They operate illegal hunting camps, illegal air taxi operations, and illegal backpacking trips within the park's boundaries. Due to a shortage of manpower, it is extremely difficult to stop these illegal activities. The park lacks a sufficient law enforcement staff to adequately patrol the area's eight plus million acres.

Another wildlife violation violates the Airborne Hunting Act. Hunters pursue, harass, and shoot game from airplanes. This is illegal in Alaska. In Wrangell St. Elias it is particularly a problem concerning the hunting of wolves. There is a push on in the state to control the wolf as a predator, according to Wells. The state and its hunter groups think that it is necessary to keep the wolves from eating so many moose and caribou. These are important species for the sport hunting industry. They are putting a lot of pressure on the state legislature to control the wolves. The state is planning to make the shooting of wolves from the air legal; however, it is not legal to do so in the park or the preserve now. Yet according to Wells, they have people who will shoot them right in the park. Wells states, "On a sunny day, right after a fresh dump of snow, they will cut them (wolves) out of a pack and run them until they are so exhausted that they can just shoot them out of the back seat of a SuperCub with a shotgun or an automatic rifle, or run a wolf... then land next to it on skis and shoot him in the head with a .22. That is what's happening."

Last year the park made a case against some wolf poachers in the southern portion of the park. Poachers were killing wolves and wolverines by running them with airplanes; however, the rangers couldn't prove it. The poachers were convicted under the Lacey Act and the case was plea bargained.

Wells says that wolf hunting is a real passion in Alaska. When there were bounties on the animals, hunters would shoot eight to ten wolves a day. He also states that individuals are demanding that the National Park Service do predator control within the park. Jay also states that park policy prevents managing one species over another. The national parks are places where natural processes are allowed to run their course.

One very interesting poaching case at Wrangell St. Elias involved a big game hunt for Dall sheep. Legal Dall sheep hunts sell for $8,000. Illegal hunts for trophy rams can sell for as much as $25,000 to $100,000. These illegal outfitters may use several airplanes, a radio scrambler program, and camouflage gear. The park hires extra help when the hunting season begins in order to combat these illegal operations. They also work closely with the United States Fish and Wildlife Service agents. They engage in joint patrols with the Kiwani Park wardens in Canada and the Yukon conservation officers. All these law enforcement officers concentrate their activities in areas that have seen a lot of poaching activity in the past. Wells states, "We could use ten more rangers and three or four airplanes. The budget keeps diminishing each year. In 1982, we had 14 seasonal law enforcement rangers; in 1993 we only had one." The park needs seasonal rangers who are continuously in the backcountry watching and listening for illegal activities. Manpower is the key deterrent in fighting poachers. Fish and wildlife law enforcement agency directors have ranked increased manpower as the most effective and desirable method to reduce violations (Nelson and Verbyla).

— Real Life Situation ———————————————————

When asked for a particular incident which could serve as an example of severe violations, Wells told this story:

The Fish and Wildlife Service agents were working on a large wildlife case in the northern part of the state, and as part of that case, they executed a search warrant and seized hunting photographs. One of the agents thought he recognized the background of a picture which showed the suspect holding up a trophy Dall sheep. A Dall sheep had been reported illegally taken.

This agent thought the mountains looked like they part of the Wrangell Mountains, so he sent the picture there. Some rangers thought they recognized the background and later flew around this area and located the right spot from the background peaks in the picture. It was in a very inaccessible place. A few weeks later a helicopter was in the park doing some other work so it was diverted there for an afternoon. It took two officers in there and set them down. They walked around and located the site where they could exactly line up the picture. In fact, they took another picture with the ranger posing as this guy holding up a pack like the sheep. If the two pictures are compared, they appear identical. The rangers looked around but couldn't find any physical evidence. They continued looking, when finally a ranger who was digging in a crevasse near a rock, pulled some rocks out, and saw some sheep's hair. After digging further, he found a skull plate and the remains of the sheep. This kill occurred inside the park, and the guy who took it was not eligible to take it by subsistence hunting regulations.

As a result of this find, they got a search warrant from the court and seized the Dall sheep head and charged the suspect with illegal hunting in the park and transporting it. The defendant pled out on the charges. He lost a couple of airplanes and received jail time and a big fine. The Fish and Wildlife Service confiscated the sheep head, of course, and presented it to their superintendent at a law enforcement meeting. It was displayed in our visitors center with a placard on it explaining that it was taken illegally.

About a month later, the visitor's center was broken into. It was a forcible entry, and the sheep head was stolen. Nothing else was stolen. It has not been recovered.

The outlook is not good. Alaska will continue to be hampered by poachers and other illegal wildlife activities until the law enforcement agencies are beefed up and budgets allow the employment of an adequate number of officers. Any kind of effort to increase law enforcement activities in Alaska are quickly met with objections from some of the congressional delegation.

These are not the only problems concerning poachers in our parks. Great Basin National Park, our newest park, experiences a different type of poaching violation. Jim Unruh, the law enforcement specialist at Great Basin National Park, relates that poaching goes on regularly within its boundaries. The area around this park is a very popular area for big game hunting. People have hunted the land that makes up the park until it was named a national park in 1986. Great Basin was once Lehman Caves National Monument. The National Park was renamed, and it was enlarged by acquisition of former National Forest Service land. These lands were historically used for big game hunting. Rangers have overheard hunters commenting that, "My father hunted here, my grandfather hunted here, by gosh, I'm going to hunt here." This fact is also complicated by a shortage of manpower. The people never see a ranger in this park's backcountry, so there is no one to stop the illegal hunting. It just continues unabated. Some of the poachers even use park roads to get to legal hunting areas, then transport their game back across the park, while carrying loaded uncased weapons in their vehicles. The best way to control this problem is through education.

Big game animals are not the only wildlife which are taken illegally within the boundaries of the national parks. Jay Liggett, the Flamingo District Ranger at the Everglades National Park, reports that illegal mullet fishing is a serious problem there. The mullets are highly desired because of their roe. The Japanese treasure this species. Because of the pressure being put on this species by Japanese buyers, the price increases. The mullet school in the waters of the Everglades National Park and when they school, they can be easily captured with a boat and a net. Poachers can easily make between $5,000 and $10,000 a night. Most of these poaching incidents have occurred in the Northwest District of the park. A deterrent program is necessary if we, as rangers, will succeed in the prevention of poaching in our parks.

Not all of the poaching incidents are wildlife related. Plants can also be poaching victims. Karen Ardoin, Chief Ranger at Haleakala National Park in Hawaii, talked about their Japanese visitors and the poaching of rare plants. Japanese visitors culturally have a habit of taking plants home as gifts. It is not uncommon for the agricultural inspectors at the Haleakala Airport to give the rangers a call, saying that they have some Silver Swords. The Silver Sword is a plant found only on Maui, and it is a threatened plant. Usually the roots have been damaged enough so that they can't be saved. The visitor is ticketed and fined for picking this plant. It is the same as poaching. Everything in the National Park is protected, and it is so fundamental that only a ticket gets the message across, according to Ardoin. The park experiences multilingual problems, and they can't make Japanese signs. The park's interpretive division is working with commercial use permittees. This is a plausible solution. Through interpretation and the cooperation with the concessionaires that bring the Japanese tourists, an educational process could be targeted at the prevention of plant poaching by foreign visitors.

Gunnysacks are all that a poacher needs if his target is mushrooms. Crater Lake National Park contains a very special mushroom, the mockatossi mushroom. According to Steve Gough, the Red Cone Area Ranger at Crater Lake National Park, they are highly prized in the Orient. People illegally pick these mushrooms in the park. Gough says that people are allowed to pick them in adjacent national forest lands with a permit, although it is not allowed upon national park land. These mushrooms will sell for anywhere from $20 to $300 a pound locally. A lot more money can be made if you can find a Japanese buyer. Gough states that they catch people while they are in the park with the mushrooms, then seize the mushrooms and any of the tools which were used to harvest the mushrooms. In minor cases, this usually involves a citation; however, in a major harvest of these mushrooms, arrests have been made.

Compliance with our laws and regulations is the mission of all law enforcement rangers; this can be achieved through various methods. One way of gaining compliance is through the utilization of information from the general public. The visitors to all of our parks should be encouraged to report anything which seems strange and out of the ordinary.

Roger Semler, the wilderness ranger for Glacier National Park totally agrees. He states that poaching is a large concern in Glacier because they have a very rich wildlife resource. He also says that the park is very vulnerable because they have a large boundary to patrol. The trophy size animals within the park attract the "wildlife crime people." He goes on to say that the rangers in Glacier do not make many "cases" every year because of a lack of manpower. He states that six cases involving wildlife crimes were handled in 1992. If the public visiting in our parks would be observant and report all the violations that they see, perhaps the number of violations arrested for or cited would increase.

Semler related that two years ago in 1991, a couple of individuals killed a nanny mountain goat alongside Highway Two near an area called the "Goat Lick." This violation was reported and the individuals were apprehended. In the course of the investigation and apprehension, the weapon which was used and the vehicle belonging to the individuals were both seized and, ultimately, the vehicle and weapon were forfeited to the government, along with some heavy monetary penalties. The Park Service in the Glacier area usually asks for and receives pretty stiff sentences for its wildlife convictions. This is meant to serve as a deterrent to other violators. If the war on poaching is to be won in our national parks, judges and prosecutors must treat wildlife offenses as serious offenses. One of the key components in this fight is to educate our magistrates and prosecutors about the serious consequences to our wildlife populations in the parks.

— Real Life Situation —————————

According to Larry L. Hakel, Chief Ranger at Shenandoah National Park, some violators helped in their own apprehension. A group of hunters, illegally hunting with dogs in the park, videotaped their entire hunt. This included the treeing of a park black bear and the shooting of the bear. The rangers seized the video when they arrested the poachers. The video was used to convict the members of the group.

Poaching cases in our parks are rampant. Dee Renee Ericks (now at Olympic National Park) arrested an adult and a juvenile, while working as a ranger in the Great Smoky Mountains National Park, for trying to abduct three bear cubs. The mother bear had been killed by the pair. The cubs were taken by park rangers and introduced to a surrogate mother bear. The adult was charged and convicted, he paid a heavy fine, spent five months and 29 days in jail, and both he and the juvenile did community service for the violation. In addition, both lost their state hunting and fishing privileges. In the Olympic National Park, where Ericks now works, special hunting patrols are organized. These patrols are important especially during the elk hunting season. The rangers also do stakeouts utilizing fake deer. A special emphasis is placed on boundary patrols.

William Sigler, in his book *Wildlife Law Enforcement,* states, "The underlying philosophy of modern law enforcement procedures stresses compliance with the law, not because of fear of punishment but because of an enlightened self-interest growing out of a program of public information." The ranger must be prepared to explain to the potential violator the reasons why not to poach in the park. If this information is coupled with more officer presence, compliance would be easier to gain. Backcountry patrols should be initiated in some areas and increased in others. Patrols will catch violators. There is also a need for more information. Research suggests that the trailhead is an appropriate place for this information concerning poaching and boundaries. I believe that increased hunter education at a younger age would also aid in solving the problem with hunter ignorance, however not with a "diehard" poacher.

It may be time for nontraditional methods. Methods which were developed by the U.S. Fish and Wildlife Agent Dave Hall. Dave Hall uses chronic wildlife violators as assistants in spreading the message against poaching. Dave has recruited convicted violators. These convicted poachers make public appearances in their local communities and tell the hunting and fishing public what poaching does to fragile wildlife populations. They also appear on television and their stories have appeared in nationally published sportsmen magazines. Hall also uses videotaped interviews of these violators, telling others the harm poaching really does cause. He utilizes the videos on his speaking tours. These methods should be adopted by rangers in order to combat poaching by local residents. These local residents are part of a larger poaching problem in many other parks, that of commercial poaching operations.

A deterrent philosophy needs to be implemented by the National Park Service. Dave Hall has implemented a deterrent philosophy which links certain elements together to gain or improve compliance with the law. These links, according to Hall, are:

1. Simple and understandable laws.

2. Offenders who have the greatest impact on wildlife should be concentrated on by the rangers, not the minor offenders.

3. A healthy respect should exist for wildlife laws by judges and prosecutors, they should fully prosecute violators.

4. Sentences for violations should produce the greatest deterrent effect possible (e.g., revocation of hunting privileges, forfeiture of equipment, jail time and heavy fines.

5. The public should be educated in the importance of wildlife laws.

6. If the first five links are strong, eventually they will aid in changing public attitudes and behavior.

This type of deterrent philosophy could work in all national parks.

Law enforcement rangers must assume the leadership in educating all individuals about our wildlife laws and regulations in order to gain compliance. If education falls short of its mark, then other means must be employed to combat poaching in the parks. Most poachers fear the loss of their hunting rights the most. Therefore, these rights should be revoked in order to serve as a deterrent to other would-be violators. If this doesn't work, more drastic measures can be taken. Measures, such as sentences of community service, where the offender does community work while publicly visible, and the confiscation of vehicles and equipment, would certainly send a clear message to other poachers. Finally, if all this still fails, then the wildlife poacher should be incarcerated. Certain magistrates have established new innovative types of incarceration, such as a holiday or weekend lock down, where the offender is locked up during the time he/she would ordinarily spend in the field.

Before any of the deterrent methods will give relief to the problem, we must have officials who are willing to prosecute and sentence violators. Federal magistrates must understand the serious consequences of a failure to protect wildlife in our parks. Go out and convince your magistrate that what you have in your national park is worth preserving. Remind him or her of what is stated in the Organic Act of 1916. Our mission is to conserve and protect for current and future generations! We cannot do our job unless they also do their job. This is true for all of the arrests and citations we issue for all the various violations which occur in the National Park System.

References

Borrelli, P., "On Poaching" *The Amicus Journal*. 10 (2):2, 1988.

Gray, B.T., "Illegal Waterfowl Hunting in The Mississippi Flyway and Recommendations for Alleviation." Ph.D. Thesis. Mississippi State University, 1992.

Hall, D.L. ,"Using the Video Camera to Educate Duck Hunters." The International Waterfowl Symposium. 6: 249-260, 1989.

Jackson, R., R. Norton and R. Anderson,"Improving Ethical Behavior in Hunters," Trans North American Wildlife Resource Conference. 44:306-318, 1979.

Nelson, C. and D. Verbyla, "Characteristics and Effectiveness of State Anti-Poaching Campaigns." *Wildlife Society Bulletin*, 12 (2) : 117-122, 1984.

_____, "Hunter Compliance in North America: Past, Present, and Future." International Conference of Improving Hunter Compliance with Wildlife Laws, 1:21-35, 1992.

_____"Compliance Presentation," Reno, Nevada Conference of Parks Law Enforcement Association, 1993.

CHAPTER 9

OFF–ROAD VEHICLE VIOLATIONS

O   ff-road vehicle violations were reported to be major
         violations in 55 percent of the 29 national parks in
         which rangers were interviewed.

Off-road vehicle (ORV) is defined by Robert Rasor of the
American Motorcyclist Association as:

> Any vehicle designed for, or capable of, travel on
> or immediately over land, water, sand, snow, ice,
> marsh, swampland, or other natural terrain, including
> but not limited to: automobiles, trucks, four-wheel
> drive or low-pressure tire vehicles, motorcycles,
> trailbikes, snowmobiles, amphibious machines,
> ground-effect or air-cushion vehicles, recreation camp-
> ers, and any other means of transportation deriving
> motive force other than muscle.

The term ORV will be used in this chapter to describe all
operations of wheeled vehicles off of designated roads and trails.
(For our purposes, I shall include muscle propelled vehicles, such
as mountain bikes and other bicycle type conveyances.)

OFF-ROAD VEHICLE USE

All vehicle use within our National Park System is relegated
to use on paved roads only, except where particular parks have
made exceptions, such as the use of snowmobiles in Voyageur
National Park. The use and operation of ORVs has become an
important part of outdoor recreation. This poses a serious conflict.

ORV operators think of their machines as a means to enjoyment. Rangers believe the machines cause considerable impact on the land, vegetation, wildlife, and other park visitors.

The conflicts are often inevitable between ORV users and other recreationists who are seeking the solitude of our national park backcountry. The velocity and noise created by these vehicles can be invasive. I was involved in an investigation of an ORV violation that culminated after two years of time and trouble.

— Real Life Situation ———————————

The case involved individuals from a private area adjacent to the Coulee Dam National Recreation Area who would use the park as an ORV racetrack. The adults from this private area rode their ORVs through an adjacent NPS campground. These same individuals encouraged the use of park property by their children and their mini ORVs. I was aware of this illegal use, but I was not able to personally observe these violations. It wasn't until one day in August 1992 that I caught three juveniles using their makeshift racetrack. I cited the responsible adults with a mandatory appearance in court. The individuals were charged with destroying vegetation on park lands and for riding off of designated park roads. The individual was convicted of the violation and fined accordingly.

In some cases, the magistrates have thrown these cases out of court because the magistrate does not realize the seriousness of the impacts caused by these machines. Even pedaled mountain bikes can cause very serious erosion and soil compaction in areas of our backcountry.

A common solution outside of national parks is called zoning. This simply separates an area according to its use. The solution within the parks is simply to exclude all use of ORVs. In 1972, President Nixon issued an Executive Order governing the use of ORVs on public land. Executive Order 11644 stated that government agencies shall establish policies and procedures to ensure that ORV use on public land is controlled and directed so as to protect natural resources; to promote the safety of all users of these lands; and to minimize conflict among land uses. The U.S. Forest Service and the BLM deemed it an acceptable use of some of their lands, the NPS deemed it an unacceptable use for lands under their jurisdiction, with the exception of snowmobiling. Snowmobiling has been allowed on unplowed winter roads in many parks including Yellowstone.

The use of snowmobiles has promoted damage to vegetation and soils, especially in areas where the snow cover is light. Because of these problems and the noise, misbehavior and wildlife harassment, snowmobilers were outlawed from Glacier National Park in 1975. Voyageur National Park has also found itself embroiled in a conflict over the establishment of snowmobile trails through a proposed wilderness area on Kabetogoma Peninsula within the park's boundaries.

According to the chief ranger of Voyageur National Park, Bruce Mckeeman, the use of that area by snowmobilers has been a traditional use. It is now causing a great deal of conflict because the area which has been used is a proposed wilderness area. Another problem in Voyageurs is the use of snowmobiles by intoxicated operators. The rangers in Voyageurs National Park patrol the snowmobile trails, much the same way as state troopers patrol the highways watching for drunk drivers. These intoxicated individuals pose a great harm for other operators, and they also damage the resources due to their careless operation.

Many accounts of serious violations have been related to me by various rangers in the American Southwest. Chief Ranger Dale Antonich of Lake Mead National Recreation Area, tells this story about ORV misuse:

> The biggest thing is the off-road abuse of the backcountry. We have roads spiraling off in all areas of the park. The fishermen think that they can go down to the lake at any point they want. They find a better cove so they just make another new road to it. This past year, we had significant off road damage up in Colville

Bay. The aircraft saw the individual off road. The pilot alerted the rangers who got in position, and then herded the guy out of the backcountry. The suspect thought he was escaping, but the plane chased him into the waiting rangers. They road blocked him in and arrested him. That individual procured a ton of damage; the judge literally 'hammered' him. He was ordered to do 250 hours of community service for the Park Service, and he is specifically designated to rake out the off-road vehicle tracks he made. These hours were to be served during the summer months during the hours of 5 a.m. and 8 P.M. The judge fined him on two different violation notices—$550 on one and $250 on another one. His drivers license was already in suspension by the state. The judge did everything he could to punish him because it was blatant. He rode over an area where there are Bear Paw Poppies, which are protected. Resource management staff evaluated the cost to rehabilitate that area. The guy was also ordered to pay the NPS $2800.00 worth of rehab damages, which was just enough money to buy all the plants. The suspect had to replant them himself.

Tony Schetzsle, the chief ranger from Canyon Lands National Park, reports many off-road violations. Tony says that the problem in his park is pervasive, because there is so much access to the backcountry by four-wheel drive roads. He states that the rangers have no direct control over this access. This poses a problem for Canyon Land rangers. The park uses a backcountry permit system. Anyone who spends the night in the park's backcountry is required to have a permit. The problem lies with the fact that there are too many backcountry access roads to patrol, so the ranger staff has no idea who is where, or even if those individuals have permits. Some of these access roads are truly four-wheel drive roads. Given the nature of these roads, they are also suitable for mountain bikes, and the mountain bikers are restricted to these roads and these roads alone. No specially designated trails have been set aside primarily for mountain bikes. This has also posed a problem. Once these bikers head out on one of these roads, they tend to branch out and go off of established roadways causing damage to the area.

According to Schetzsle, this is one of the primary violations in the park. However, it is not necessarily a problem exclusive to mountain biking, it concerns the use of off-road motorcycles and four-wheel drive vehicles also. If something looks interesting to one of these visitors, instead of getting out of their vehicle and walking up to the interesting feature, they just drive their vehicle up to the object. This causes severe impacts in this fragile desert ecosystem. The rangers in Canyon Lands National Park spend quite a bit of time raking out vehicle tracks. If, according to the chief ranger, you consider the tremendous increase in visitation to the park over the last 12 years, it is a very severe impact on the resource. The park saw visitation figures rise from 40,000 in 1980 to 400,000 in 1992. When I visited the park in 1993, I saw a mountain bike or two on every other vehicle. I was amazed at the number of off-road vehicles. The average backcountry recreationist has a strong aversion to any kind of vehicle in the backcountry. All of these different interests are sure to create conflict situations.

The traditional backcountry recreationist and the off-road vehicle visitor both require a great deal of space. The traditional visitor requires solitude and serenity, which the off-road vehicle user may not respect. Due to legal mandates, the traditional type of solitude is what will be provided in our national parks. The ORV visitor will have to go elsewhere to enjoy his type of recreation.

OFF-ROAD IMPACT

Various studies have indicated that impacts on desert lands from ORVs are very serious. The ecosystem of our desert backcountry areas is very fragile. Knudson has documented the following impacts in desert country by ORVs:

1. Direct killing of plants and animals

2. Crushing of ground nests and breaking of shrubs with bird nests

3. Collapsed burrows

4. Harassment, producing an energy strain in an environment of high stress (e.g., incubating birds may abandon nests)

5. Vegetation indirectly destroyed by crushing and exposure of shallow roots, leading to deprivation of food and cover for animals and birds

6. Mechanical disturbance of the soil upsets water storage, reduces water infiltration capacity, changes the thermal structure of the soil, and disrupts germination strategies of seeds, reducing the number of spring annuals

These are some very strong arguments to eliminate the use of ORVs from our national parks and possibly from all other public lands, especially in fragile desert ecosystems.

EDUCATION

VISITOR

When you encounter these visitors, keep in mind that their violations may be unintentional. The conflicts between these violators and rangers may be minimized if the ranger explains the reason for not operating ORVs off of park roads. Remember that education is the ranger's best tool. Some suggestions may be to use better signage; include the regulations against the use of ORVs in the park's brochures; and utilize the expertise of the park's interpretive staff to get the message out.

Jay Liggett states that one of the most serious problems in the Everglades National Park backcountry is boat groundings. He says that boats and airboats tend to destroy the seagrass. Liggett poses a unique quandary, if a vehicle runs off the road and hits a tree, the person is not cited for destroying natural features, but in the Everglades when a boater goes aground, he/she is cited for damaging natural features. This type of damage is a very severe impact on the park's vegetation. Liggett goes on to say that this type of misuse causes considerable problems in areas that most rangers would never think about. It will change the PH of the sediment in the soil as the layers move down. Once the PH is changed, the seagrass will not grow there. If the bank is gouged by a vessel, the tide begins to erode away at the bank, then before long it's not a bank, it's a new channel. It is not just a minor problem, it is a serious violation that must be solved through enforcement and education. Education can consist of just a simple resource message given to the visitor by the ranger. Liggett says, "It is a learning process for our magistrates and justice system, and we seem to be making progress." In the Everglades, like Lake Mead, deterrence is a good method to end these problems. The more convictions we obtain for good ORV cases, the less violations we will encounter in the future.

Chief Ranger Charlie Peterson of Bryce Canyon National Park, suggests that all rangers be armed with simple resource messages about the most serious problems in their particular backcountry area. The majority of problems which occur in Bryce concern visitors from foreign countries, namely visitors from Germany and Japan. If the resource message is printed in the visitor's language, then the individual cannot just give you a blank stare. Sometimes these individuals understand the message you are giving them but fail to respond on purpose. If this type of literature is used, then the individuals are sure to "get the message." It may be expensive, but the resource is worth the expense, especially if the violations are largely from a particular source, foreign visitors.

In some parks, such as Haleakala National Park in Hawaii, it is even harmful to walk off of the trails, let alone drive off the roads. Karen Ardoin states that the reasons for keeping everyone on the roads are many, including: several endangered insect species, the disturbance of archaeological features, and even moving rocks can change the ecosystem, which is so very fragile. The only way to deter some visitors from violating the rules is to enforce the regulations very literally and strictly. In other parks the problem isn't just keeping visitors on the trail; it is keeping them on a road.

COURT OFFICIALS

According to Antonich, rangers need to tell magistrates why they are there. They are there to protect the natural resources. They need to educate the magistrates and the U.S. attorneys. This is why the National Park Service has law enforcement rangers. At Lake Mead, they get magistrates and U.S. attorneys out on the water and up in the air; they fly them all over and let them see first-hand what's going on in the park. The rangers also take them out on the lake for a day in the boat. It is relaxing to them, and they get a better understanding of what is going on. This whole process has taken years to accomplish. But educating all factions of the public is worthwhile.

References

Baldwin, M. and D. Stoddard, Jr. *The Off-Road Vehicle and Environmental Quality. 2nd.* ed. (Washington D.C.: The Conservation Foundation) 1973.

Douglas, R., *Forest Recreation* (Prospect Heights, IL: Waveland Press) 1993.

Knudson, D., *Outdoor Recreation* (NY: Macmillan Publishing Co.) 1984.

Lucas, R., *Hikers and Other Trail Users*, Proceedings of the Recreation Symposium (Upper Darby, PA: Northeast Forest Experiment Station) 1971.

Rasor, R., *Five State Approaches to Trailbike Recreation Facilities and Their Management* (Westerville, OH: American Motorcyclist Association) 1977.

CHAPTER 10

ARCHAEOLOGICAL RESOURCE PROTECTION

The mission of the National Park Service instructs us to protect cultural objects. These objects can also be archaeological resources. Archaeological resource violations were reported to be major violations in 28 percent of the 29 national parks in which interviews of rangers were conducted.

ARCHAEOLOGICAL RESOURCES

According to the Archaeological Resource Protection Act, (Title 16 USC section 470bb) the term *archaeological resource* means:

> Any material remains of past human life or activities which are of archaeological interest, as determined under uniform regulations promulgated pursuant to this act. Such regulations containing such determination shall include, but not be limited to: pottery, basketry, bottles, weapons, weapon projectiles, tools, structures, or portions of structures, pit houses, rock paintings, rock carvings, intaglios, graves, human skeletal materials, or any portion or piece of any of the foregoing items. Non-fossilized and fossilized paleontological specimens, or any portion or piece thereof, shall not be considered archaeological resources, under the regulations under this paragraph, unless found in an archaeological context. No item shall be treated as an archaeological resource under this regulation unless such item is at least 100 years of age.

RESOURCE PROTECTION

Why should we protect such resources? These resources are an irreplaceable part of our nation's heritage. They are becoming increasingly endangered because of their attractiveness as a commercial resource. They can be sold for large amounts of money in certain circles, both legally and illegally. The uncontrolled excavation and pillage of these resources results in a loss of knowledge of our past. Artifacts and resources in private possession are not available for public display and knowledge. In order to secure these resources for the American public's future benefit, the National Park Service law enforcement ranger must protect the archaeological resources and sites found in our national parks.

Many people are disturbing and taking the resources which the Archaeological Resource Protection Act protects. Many people participating in these violations are either not informed of the illegalities or they consider the law to be oppressive, invalid or unnecessary. These types of people believe that this law was never meant to be enforced; they have what some people call the "finders keeper" mentality. This is especially true with a resource that has monetary value, and the prohibition against the taking of them is ignored.

There are many violators of this law. Some are everyday people, others are university students and experts in the field of archaeology. Tony Schetzsle from Canyon Lands describes one university group like this:

> We had an incident a year and a half ago involving a father/son outing from a number of universities. In the Horseshoe Canyon unit of the park, we have rock art sites that are the big arch types. In the presence of their father, who sat there and watched, two juveniles etched their names in these alcoves where the rock panels exist. That's an example of vandalism.
>
> We are trying to educate these people as they come into the park. Because of the problem with access to the park, there are many people we will never see

until they are in the park and a backcountry ranger contacts them. If they are overnight visitors, we will get a chance to contact them. When we encounter these flagrant violations, we are unforgiving. Somebody will be left with a hard copy, if not a notice to appear based upon information or a grand jury indictment.

VIOLATORS

There are many other violators, including dealers, vandals, looters, collectors, artifact hunters, and visitors. Dealers are those persons engaged in buying and selling valuable artifacts. Some of these individuals are especially gifted in tracing the origin of a certain object and determining the legality of its possession. Others are more concerned with making a profit and with the objects saleability. Some dealers are so unscrupulous that they will even encourage others to do their looting for them.

Vandals are persons who deliberately deface and destroy some item of archaeological value. The use of off-road vehicles in archaeological sites is a prime example of this type of vandalism. It is a total disregard for these precious articles of antiquity. Other vandals may shoot at rock art or purposely dismantle archaeological structures.

Looters are persons who make a living from selling archaeological objects which they have dug up and removed. These items are usually sold to the aforementioned unscrupulous dealers. These violators are usually very knowledgeable about the site locations and the types of items which can be found. It is not uncommon to find looters with college educations in archaeology.

Collectors are persons who enjoy possessing and displaying archaeological resources. Some of these individuals are interested in the items' historical aspects, some in the items' artistic aspect and others are only interested because the object has value. Some of these individuals purchase objects from dealers, others directly from the looter.

Artifact hunters are individuals who might also be known as amateur archaeologists. Their hobby is treasure hunting. Most fathom themselves to be like their movie hero "Indiana Jones."

This is a recreational pursuit for these individuals. It involves searching for arrowheads, bottles, coins, bullets, and other trinkets of antiquity. Some of these people may specialize in the civil war era, the pioneer era, or the Spanish American War. The use of the dreaded metal detector is often employed. Metal detectors are a violation of the 36 Code of Federal Regulations because of their use in obtaining artifacts.

Finally, visitors who visit sites for recreational purposes may see an opportunity to pickup a souvenir and pocket an artifact. This is probably the simplest ARPA violation which you may encounter. The solution to this type of violation is simply education. Tell the visitor the rule, explain it, and then tell them again.

The following case is an ongoing problem for the National Park Service.

– Real Life Situation ————————————

There are many archaeological sites on the Coulee Dam National Recreation Area. Fortunately, many are located under Lake Roosevelt. When the Grand Coulee Dam was built, it backed up the waters of the Columbia River and formed Lake Roosevelt. These waters covered the sites of old Kettle Falls and other important archaeological sites. The waters did not cover the site of Fort Spokane. Fort Spokane is the location of a military post erected to protect the eastern portion of the state of Washington in the late 1800s. The problem lies with the dump site at the old fort. This dump contains artifacts from the infantry and cavalry era of the last century. The Park Service has been having problems with people looting this dump site and removing valuable artifacts. The exact location of this site is not public information, yet the looting continues.

The National Park Service utilizes three different protection techniques to safeguard sites such as this "dump"—protection, investigation and education.

The protection itself consists of various methods such as knowing the exact location of the sites; maintaining good site inventories; erecting gates, signs, and fences; conducting patrols and maintaining surveillance; monitoring visitor patterns; using volunteers, informants, and a reward system; and the use of detection devices. Each form of protection lends itself to a particular site. One method may be appropriate in one location but not appropriate for another location. Each ranger in a particular district should know where these archaeological sites are located. Maps of known sites should be kept for planning and scheduling patrols of the areas. These maps should not be displayed on walls but should be kept confidential.

Each known archaeological site should have a physical inventory list prepared and kept on file. The list should also contain a rough sketch of the major features and of the existing damage and defacement which may be present on the site. Photographs should be included with this list as well. It is important to have a baseline of the site in order to make comparisons if further damage occurs.

Signs should be placed at these sites. These signs should inform the visitor of the prohibitions concerning the site. In some cases, caution is advised, the sign itself may draw public attention to the site. Fences and gates could be used to prevent crimes of opportunity and to prevent the driving of vehicles onto the site.

Regular and recurring patrols should be scheduled for all known sites. The times of these patrols should also be varied. All patrol schedules must be kept confidential. If the site is so far in the backcountry that a physical inspection is not possible, then a fly over patrol should be scheduled.

All visitor use patterns must be monitored. The ranger can use traffic counters, entrance stations, contact points or patrol logs to determine if a site is threatened. These methods will also be useful in predicting periods of heavy visitation. During those periods, ranger presence should be increased.

The help of volunteers can also be enlisted, along with the use of informants and rewards. Volunteers can be used for monitoring patrols, site mapping and taking inventory. In these days of low budgets and a lack of manpower, they can be an excellent alternative to hiring more rangers. Use the help of local residents who may live near the accessible sites. These individuals can provide the ranger with information on vehicle types, license numbers, and times. ARPA authorizes the payment of rewards for information leading to the arrest and conviction of violators, so utilize every tool you may have at your disposal.

Finally, detection devices may also be used to detect an unwanted presence at a site. Motion detectors could be used to trigger hidden cameras and set off an alarm at the dispatcher's office. If this option is not available to you, consider the use of signs stating that an alarm system is in place even if no system exists. This may also serve as a deterrent. Be aware that this may also draw attention to a site.

In the backcountry, many archaeological violations are crimes of opportunity. A visitor happens upon a site, which may or may not be known to the park officers, the visitor notices pieces of pottery, or whatever, and just helps him or herself. The solution to this type of violation is education. Tell the visitor that all archaeological or paleontological objects must be left where they are found. Inform them of the value of the object, if it is in its original location. If the item is removed, even if its brought to you, its original value will be lost. To take an object out of its location is detrimental to the location and the object. Inform the visitor through interpretation, signs, personal contact, and if the occasion arises, through law enforcement.

Other national parks reporting vandalism and theft of archaeological resources include, but are not limited to, Haleakala National Park in Hawaii and Great Basin National Park in Nevada. Haleakala reports that visitors commonly take whatever resources may be readily taken without detection. These are definitely crimes of opportunity. A few extra precautions, such as an added patrol, on the part of the ranger staff could eliminate crimes of opportunity (e.g., park an extra patrol vehicle near an access trail to an archaeological resource). This may serve as a deterrent to anyone who would seize the moment and steal a resource.

Great Basin National Park in Nevada reports that archaeological resource vandalism is often committed by the many boy scout troops that visit the park. Often, the scouts are not fully informed about the valuable resources within the parks. Jim

Unruh says, "This park has more vandalism than any other park I have worked in." The worse form of this occurs with some of the park's archaeological resources in the park's backcountry. Great Basin rangers utilize educational messages posted on signs at trailheads. If visitors are seen by the rangers, they approach the visitor and give them verbal messages concerning the resources. They definitely go out of their way to contact all of the boy scout troops utilizing the park. Education sometimes is not enough, at times it must be supplemented with the weight of law. Citations may sometimes get a message across to an individual when other methods fail.

INVESTIGATION

If archaeological resources are vandalized, stolen or destroyed, then law enforcement rangers are called upon to investigate these occurrences. All archaeological resource damage cases deserve a thorough investigation no matter how insignificant the case may appear. If successful prosecution is expected, then a thorough search of the crime scene must be conducted as soon after the discovery of the crime as possible. A National Park Service archaeologist must be consulted and used to assist in the crime scene search, site sketching, documentation, the identification of the evidence, and the assessment of the damage. The archaeologist will become the expert witness in any archaeological resource case.

Photographs of the damage must be taken and properly recorded. This also illustrates the importance of baseline photos which should be kept on file. With these photographs as a baseline, comparisons can be made. Evidence must be collected at the scene. The archaeologist may be helpful in determining evidence in these types of cases.

An accurate case report, including all collected materials, initial reports, sketches, photos, damage assessments, evidence logs, suspect identification, witness identification, and qualifications of the archaeologist, must be prepared by the ranger. Writing skills are of great importance to the law enforcement ranger. You must have these skills well developed in order to write an accurate report in a case of this nature.

A damage assessment should be written for all cases in order to determine the $500 threshold for prosecution as a felony and for collection of civil damages. This can be done even if there is not enough evidence for criminal prosecution.

If the vandalism or theft is an ongoing situation and you are unable through the collection of evidence to apprehend a suspect, consider an undercover operation. Use a plain clothes ranger to pose as a dealer or collector in order to make a buy, determine target locations, or to develop more probable cause in order to obtain a search warrant. Always be aware of the suspect's Fourth Amendment rights when making seizures. The authority to seize archaeological resources is based upon probable cause that such resources came from national park lands or other public lands. Most searches for these items occur at private residences or museums; therefore, the search warrant is a requirement. The resources of the entire federal law enforcement system are usually at the disposal of the ranger in most serious cases.

— Real Life Situation

I'll never forget one case that occurred in Death Valley. I was in the area near the Race Track Plya; it was late spring and the weather was getting pretty warm. Death Valley has a history of outlaw motorcycle gangs coming through the park. I had never met an outlaw dune buggy gang, however, not until that day. About a dozen dune buggies came rolling up, driven by people who looked just like outlaw bikers. One of them got out and tried to introduce me to this inflatable rubber doll that he had. He wanted to know if I wanted to make love to this doll. I told him, "No thanks, you can take care of Matilda yourself." We talked a bit about where they were going and where they could and could not camp. Everything went along just fine. The contact lasted about 45 minutes. I left the area to patrol some backcountry.

I was hesitant to leave the area without checking on this group again, so I returned at the end of the day. I went to the area in which I thought they might be. As I neared the area, I started hearing gunshots, more gunshots than I ever heard in my life. They were shooting old buildings full of holes. I left the area and contacted the district ranger and tried to marshal some forces. I wanted to go in with about six rangers at about three o'clock in the morning and shake them down. The park leadership wanted to wait until the sun came up. The chief ranger wanted to fly over the site to see if these boys were still around. About an hour later, I knew these guys would be up and rested, and I didn't want to encounter them then. The chief ranger flew over them in time to see them exiting the park. I wanted to see what kind of damage they did. Later that morning, I found one entire historic structure burned to the ground. There was no physical evidence remaining.

All cases should be handled with utmost care. Complete consideration must be given to a special situations such as the one described. A surprise visit would definitely have been appropriate, and it could have saved the archaeological resources in the National Monument from destruction.

There are a lot of archaeological thefts happening at the Grand Canyon. Too often, all that is found are the dug up sites. It is very difficult to catch these violators. They know what they are looking for, they go in and dig it up, and take it with them. The biggest problem according to Chuck Sypher, is once you get a "pot" out of the park, you cannot really tell where it came from. Looters say it came from private land, and no one else can tell where it came from. Sypher states, " We come across people, now and again, who are bent over picking up pot chards. They say, "We're just looking," and "We'll put them back." Its impossible to arrest or cite these types of individuals. Once they put them in their packs, a warrant is needed. Where do you get the probable cause? Once you see these individuals and they know that a ranger is watching, they will just wait until you leave and go back and take some more chards. The fear of being detected may be the only solution to the problem in the Grand Canyon.

These problems exist in most of our scenic national parks. The National Park Service trains its rangers in the protection of archaeological resources. More information about courses offered through the National Park Service is available. The National Park Service conducts a course entitled Introduction to Archaeological Resource Protection at the Federal Law Enforcement Training Center in Georgia. The course is designed for managers and ancillary personnel to provide an awareness of the objectives and legal requirements of the Archaeological Resources Protection Act. This program is geared toward federal law enforcement officers who are employed by the federal land management agencies. It provides the basic background in archaeology that an officer needs in order to investigate resource violations. If you, as a student, are interested in this type of enforcement work, you should begin by reading more about archaeology and related fields.

References

Green, Dee and Polly Davis, "Cultural Resource Law Enforcement, An Emerging Science," (U.S. Forest Service Experimental Station, Southwest Region. Albuquerque, New Mexico) 1978.

Harden, Fred, Cultural Resources Surveillance Report: Summer 1979. Ms. report on file at B.L.M., Durango, CO.

Hutt, Sherry, Elwood Jones and Martin McAlliste, *Archaeological Resource Protection* (The Preservation Press, The National Trust for Historic Preservation) 1992.

McLane, Dennis, "Resource Protection" at the Annual PLEA Conference in Reno, Nevada, 1993.

National Park Service, U.S. Dept. of the Interior, Listings of Education in Archaeological Programs. Archaeological Assistance Program, 1992.

PL 96-95, Archaeological Resources Protection Act, 1980.

CHAPTER 11

SERIOUS CRIMINAL VIOLATIONS

T he national parks are not safe from violent criminal actions. The modern day problem of crime even follows us deep into the backcountry of our most remote park. Violent crime was reported to be a major problem in 48 percent of the 29 parks in which I conducted interviews of park rangers. The following incidents are all true and are exactly as related to me by the rangers who experienced the incidents. I will begin with the problem of youth gangs at the Lake Mead National Recreation Area.

GANGS IN THE PARKS

Chief Ranger Dale Antonich expressed grave concern for the future of Lake Mead National Recreation Area. According to Antonich, the National Recreation Area is being overrun by youthful gang members from the Las Vegas, Nevada area. Antonich tells us the following:

> We had an attempted homicide in the backcountry area. Two people were shot in their camper by an individual. Fortunately, both survived. There are multiple rapes and sexual assaults every year. They occur in the backcountry and access areas. It's remote and quiet in those areas and every year we pick up a body that is dumped in our backcountry. You never know whether they were shot there or are just dumped there at first until an autopsy has been performed.
>
> We are starting to get a lot of graffiti. This is a serious crime; a violation of the natural resources. The

163

gangs are going out and painting graffiti on the resources. They are desecrating different rock areas with
gang graffiti and tagging is going on along with that.
(*Tagging* is the process in which another gang comes
along and x's out the rival gangs graffiti.) This is
damaging our resources. We are restricting certain
areas and we run major check points with heavy patrols
where the gang activities have been in these areas. In
Clark County juveniles are prohibited by law from
possessing or buying spray paint. We enforce that, so
if they have it in their car, we seize it, and they are
written up immediately. We are doing heavy law
enforcement right now. Everybody who goes into the
backcountry is more than apt to be contacted by a
ranger. The way this park is spread out we do not utilize
a backcountry permit system. We are hoping to get
entrance stations put up in the park which will help us
control some of these access problems. Once we get
entrance stations established, we will know when
carloads of these gang bangers come into an area. Right
now, when we know where they are going to be, we
show up early in the morning and we stay there all day
long and we just hammer the heck out of them. We give
tickets to everybody for everything that we can find.
This is starting to drive them out of those areas.

   Normally, we use a five person patrol. We use
roadblocks, set up DUI checkpoints, and we check
anybody whose going in or out of the park in a typical
area where we know there are problems. We check
them for possible DUIs, weapons violations, drugs,
and spray paint.

   We ran a big operation here a couple of weeks
ago. We wrote a 150 tickets in one day. There were 24
arrests made. We had a special events team there. (A
special events team is a NPS team of law enforcement
rangers trained to handle large unruly groups.) Prior to
the King verdict, the week before we started a heavy
law enforcement operation in order to let the kids know
that this was not a place to be if there was going to be
riots. The kids from Vegas were not going to be
allowed to come out here. The local Vegas area has an
ordinance which allows only five known gang members to be together in a group. If there are more than

five, they go to jail. We get groups of 40 to 60 gang bangers at a time gathering at the park. Its a place for them to meet. These people don't camp, they come in, gather, and supposedly fish. We check them for fishing licenses, if they are fishing, but most of them are just gathering. This is a new impact on our backcountry resources. Ten years ago the gangs that came out here were outlaw motorcycle gangs. They would go to camp and mess around and party and go home.

These people are going into backcountry areas and defacing cliff faces and flat rocks. They spray paint gang graffiti on them and another group will come in there and tag that graffiti. Then you've got some real massacred areas in there.

Because this chapter includes gang-related incidents, this next threat in Zion National Park must be included.

— **Real Life Situation** ————————————

This threat was from the "Neo-Nazi" white supremist group. This group stated that they were going to claim Zion National Park as a white-only homeland. They told park authorities that they will take it over on their "day of reckoning." However, they haven't told the rangers just when that day will come.

In numerous press interviews, this group stated that their enemies will be destroyed. They list blacks, Jews, non-whites and federal law enforcement officers as their enemies. They have stated in print and on videotape that they will 'kill them all.' Another quote from this group is that 'The Virgin River will flow red with blood.' Ranger Larry Van Slyke believes that all this trouble stems from the 1970s when Zion used to be a motorcycle gang haven.

Antonich had plenty of stories to relate from his 20 years of experience with law enforcement in the national parks of our country. It is Dale's desire to help future rangers understand what faces them in today's national parks. The following two incidents, as related by Antonich, depict the criminal danger all rangers face in today's parks. He related one last incident and how a ranger copes in a high profile law enforcement park like Lake Mead. Dale told me this:

▬ Real Life Situation ━━━━━━━━━━━━━━━━

Recently, we stopped a man in the backcountry because he had a little kid sitting on his lap. The kid was driving the truck. The ranger stopped him to warn him about it. When he pulled him over, the passenger, who was a female, jumped out of the truck. She came around and started to come toward the ranger's vehicle; she had a holster on, but there was no gun in it. The ranger knew that there was probably a gun in the vehicle so he got behind his door and started giving the driver commands on the PA. The male subject rapidly bailed out of the truck and drew what turned out later to be a 357 magnum 8" barrel gun. He turned right on the ranger with it. The ranger ordered the individual to set the gun down. He put it down and the ranger arrested him when his backup showed up. They asked him why he did it, and he said, "I just don't like cops." The reason he didn't attempt to shoot the ranger was because the ranger was in a position of advantage and the guy knew it. Had it been a non-seasoned ranger who didn't know enough to realize what the situation was, the guy probably would have shot the ranger.

Antonich described the training new rangers receive when they report for work at Lake Mead National Recreation Area.

> They are assigned to field training officers for about six weeks. They don't go out on the job alone until they can prove that they can run the road alone. Even new permanent employees are assigned to a field training officer. We can't just turn green rangers loose. There is just too much intense law enforcement. After a weekend here in the summer, a new ranger has made six or eight arrests, maybe more arrests than some ranger has in his whole career. We put them through some special shooting training. They go through the regular qualifying and some tactical shooting techniques. They are drilled on approaches and car stop techniques. Its all done by the field training officer. He goes through live situations with them. We don't have the luxury of special in-service training for the seasonals. We try to bring our seasonals on for the 40-hour permanent refresher, then they train with the permanents. Lake Mead is a high profile law enforcement park. Every ranger here drives a high profile law enforcement patrol vehicle. We do more actual law enforcement than any other park in the nation!

Lake Mead was not the only park to report a real crime problem. Most of our scenic national parks had their own story to tell. In Zion National Park, Chief Ranger Larry Van Slyke reports that the serious violations include sexual assaults, assault and battery, felony theft and felony warrant arrests.

Van Slyke states that the largest portion of felony arrests rangers made in Zion National Park are associated with the Zion Lodge concession's employees. He also states that the problem is improving due to the concessionaires increased screening of new employees. The lodge hires 135 employees. All of the law enforcement problems stem from the type of person the lodge hires. He relates the following situation:

— Real Life Situation ————————

In the summer of 1992, there was an altercation between some of the lodge employees while they were working. Management indicated that they were going to dismiss one person, and they wanted rangers at the scene when that occurred because they thought that the altercation that took place was pretty serious.

The rangers found out who the individual was and ran him on the computer. The record on the guy came back five pages long. Three pages were just felony charges that had been filed against this person. He had served six years in a state penitentiary in California for rape. While in prison, he committed a rape. They also found that there was a $5,000 misdemeanor on him out of California. The person had assaulted police officers. He spent considerable time in prison. The guy was a hard core criminal. He had his rights read to him more times than our rangers have read rights to anyone. We took him into custody without incident because we had him outnumbered. It was very enlightening to see what type of people we were dealing with.

Closer to the Canadian border problems with serious crime are still the same. Tom Habeeker, Acting Chief Ranger at Denali National Park, relates this incident about a sniper in Glacier National Park.

— **Real Life Situation** —————————

He states that when he worked in Glacier he had an incident with a sniper. The man was shooting at cars and people. The person was off of the main park road and had set up camp in the backcountry. He set up in a place where he could shoot at cars without being seen by passersby. He actually hit an employee with a twenty-two calibre rifle bullet. The rangers had to close the park because of the danger from this sniper. A team of rangers and FBI agents went in, located this individual, and arrested him. It turned out that this person was wanted by the authorities in Illinois. According to another ranger in Glacier, the sniper attracted the interest of the Illinois State Bureau of Investigation who actually came to Glacier and impounded the sniper's vehicle. They took it back to Illinois in a moving van. They processed the vehicle and through the science of forensics found enough evidence to ultimately convict the Glacier sniper for the murder of a little girl in the state of Illinois. The sniper turned out to be a child killer. In a remote backcountry setting, you may some day have to deal with serious crime, perhaps homicide. Tom Habeeker puts it this way: 'The scenery is great, but you still have the same types of urban law enforcement situations in national parks that you might have elsewhere. Just because the mountains are nice, doesn't mean you [only] deal with nature walks.'

Norm Dodge of Acadia National Park relates another incident about insurance and homicide.

— **Real Life Situation** —————————

A male who worked in a paper mill put an ad in a lonely hearts column in the local newspaper. Through this ad, he met a girl. This girl was hardworking, but she was really obese. She was 26 years old. She had her own house, her own car, and some money in the bank. This person met her, and on their third date, he asked her to marry him. He told her that if she didn't, he would leave. The girl's mother and friends urged her to dump the guy, but she didn't listen to them, and she married him.

The following day they went to an insurance broker and bought a $300,000 life insurance policy on her. He also had a will written up making him the sole beneficiary. Ten days later, he pushed her off a 100 foot cliff in Acadia National Park.

We responded to that call. It was a lousy night, foggy, drizzly and cold. It was a complicated, nasty body recovery. This guy was there, and I remember standing out on the edge with him as he told me his story. Her mother called and said that it wasn't an accident and we better have a better look into this incident. It turned out to be a lengthy nine month investigation. The state police became involved with us. They made trips to Montana, where he had a previous wife who had fallen while they were out picking mushrooms. Her body was never found. He had another wife in Montana who was really afraid of him and was in hiding. The insurance agent who sold the policy had written in his notebook the fact that on a date prior to the marriage, this person came into his office and theorized that he was going to get married and he asked how much life insurance he could buy for a certain amount of money. He is now in jail.

Tony Sczhetzsle, Chief Ranger at Canyon Lands, shared this incident which occurred at Hot Springs National Park in Arkansas.

— **Real Life Situation** —————————————

This homicide occurred in the backcountry of Hot Springs National Park. The ranger was working collecting campground fees the night before this crime occurred. He remembers taking money from an elderly gentleman who was staying at the campground. The next day the man's wife reported him missing. The rangers initiated an all day search for the man. The rangers finally located the man's body on a trail a couple of days later. His head was so smashed that one of his eyes was missing. Tony said that the elderly man met another person on the trail who beat him with a rock and robbed him of twenty dollars, which was all the money the older man had on him. Tony describes the scene as brutal and gruesome. The rangers located a suspect who was later convicted of homicide.

The crimes of violence range from simple assault and rape to homicide. What causes visitors to bring their violent natures to our beautiful national parks? Perhaps no one can explain the reasons for violent crime, especially in our national park backcountry. There is one theory concerning crime in our campgrounds. Actually it is an old theory. It is the theory of social disorganization.

DISORGANIZATION IN A NATIONAL PARK SERVICE CAMPGROUND—A CASE STUDY

While the social disorganization perspective has long been associated with urban crime problems, the basic premise of the theory may also be applicable to deviant behavior in non-urban settings. The purpose of this study is to explain problems of delinquency, alcohol abuse, and other deviant behavior, which occur in a national park campground, through the theory of social disorganization.

SOCIAL DISORGANIZATION

Thomas and Znaniecki (1920) defined social disorganization as the decreasing effectiveness of control that social rules and norms have on the behavior of individuals. In an area of rapid change, where people frequently move in and out, participation in activities that do not comply with the norms and rules of the existing society are tolerated and often condoned.

Social disorganization is a child of Durkheim's theory of strain. Strain theory makes the assumption that society is an organized system, and social disorganization is a problem of the system. It is caused by rapid changes within the system. In this case, it may refer to a rapid change within an area, such as an area of transition.

Ernest Burgess stated that the typical American city, such as Chicago, takes the form of concentric zones. Zone I is the central business and industrial district. Zone II is called the transition zone, this zone is in the throes of rapid change, from residence to business. Newly arrived immigrants from the rural south as well as Europe occupy the cheap housing in the transition zone. Zone III, is where the working class lives. Zone IV and V are on the edges of the city, this is the area where the middle and upper classes live. Burgess (1926) claimed that the same general pattern appears in all major industrial centers in America, even though the industrial center may be located on the edge of a city or elsewhere.

Shaw and McKay (1942) stated that this occurs because the residential areas in the transition zone are adjacent to industrial areas and therefore are physically less desirable than those zones which are far removed. People want to live in areas which are relatively quiet and peaceful, free from pollution and stench. These industrial zones and the adjacent zone of transition were known for their traffic, noise and pollution. These zones of transition had the heaviest concentration of population. The pressure of economic competition forces the group with the lowest socioeconomic status into areas such as the transition zone, which are the least attractive. The rents in these areas are low, while economically secure groups choose higher cost residential communities, which are close to the periphery of the city. Shaw further stated that the distribution of delinquents was related to the location within the city they are in and to the composition of the population. The areas of heaviest concentration are closest to the business areas. The rates of delinquency decrease as one moves away from the city center. These zones of transition include various forms of disorganization: unemployment, dependency, misconduct, family disorganization and high rates of sickness and death (Shaw and McKay, 1942). These transition zones are characterized by a wide diversity in norms and standards of behavior. Individuals are left in confusion over what is the conventional norm and what is not acceptable. A sense of ambiguity emerges out of this disorganization. The result is an increased rate of crime in the zone of transition.

THE CAMPGROUND

The name of the campground which was studied will remain unknown, the campground is located on a man-made lake which is part of a National Recreation Area under the jurisdiction of the National Park Service. The campground receives heavy usage. The visitors come from various socioeconomic groups. The visitors are predominantly from the same state. They are, for the majority, urban dwellers. They come to this campground to spend their vacation time. It is a destination campground. Boating, fishing, swimming and other water sports are the focus activities for this campground. Normally, the months of May through August are the busiest times. The campground is patrolled by the National Park Service. A law enforcement ranger is stationed at the campground during the busiest months.

National Park Service law enforcement rangers are required to use the least restrictive method of law enforcement applicable to the situation. If their presence alone can defuse a situation, then that is *all* that is required. If this does not quell a situation, then the ranger may escalate tactics to match the situation—up to an arrest or use of deadly force. The verbal warnings issued and the informal treatment of some violations are the direct result of this low key law enforcement policy.

The campground is small; it contains 55 sites. These sites are further segmented into three parts: the loop, the overflow, and the tent only area. The loop is the original campground. It contains twenty-one sites, seven overlook the lake. All of the sites in the loop are considered very desirable by the patrons of this campground. These sites are in such high demand that campers consider obtaining a site in the loop to be a sign of a higher status. All of the sites within the campground cost $7.00 per night. Campers desiring to camp in the loop have offered the loop occupants money for their sites. Sums as high as $50 have exchanged hands for one of these favored sites.

The tent only area is an area set aside for campers camping with just tents. It is also located on the lakefront of the campground. These sites are also in high demand, although, they are not sought after in the same manner as the camp sites in the loop. The sites in the loop and in the overflow are available for use by both recreational vehicles and tents.

The overflow area was established by the Park Service because of the heavy demand for camping sites. It is basically a part of an asphalt parking lot adjacent to a strip of greenery between the marina harbor and the tent only area. It is hot and uncomfortable in the summer, and it lacks shade trees. The rules are not well defined in this area unlike the loop and the tent area where the rules are carefully posted on the camp bulletin board. The campers merely think of this camping area as a place to wait until a site is open in the loop. Because this site is on the parking lot, it receives heavy traffic during the day, and it also receives nighttime traffic as well. Travelers will pull into the parking lot at all hours and set up camp anywhere. The camp sites in the overflow are designated by yellow lines painted upon the asphalt surface. Each camper is allowed two of these parking slots and one picnic table, which is also placed upon the asphalt surface. This rule is neglected in the middle of summer. It is very difficult to monitor this campground at all times. Campers sneak in and occupy all the slots, they fail to observe the rule of not parking right next to the other site. That means instead of having 21 slots occupied in the overflow, there are over 40 sites occupied. This overflow campground is characterized by a high population density, a transient population, with a lack of rules and a sense of anonymity. This overflow area is a zone in transition.

Official occupancy figures are not available for each separate section of this campground. Only occupation figures for the entire campground are available. May through August 1992, this campground received 3,207 overnight stays from tent campers and 3,371 recreational vehicle overnight stays. The busiest month was August, it received 985 overnight tents and 999 overnight RVs (NPS,1992).

Thirty-one official violations occurred at this campground in 1992, May through August (NPS, 1992). Out of these violations 23 occurred in the transition zone. The remaining violations occurred upon park roads and in the marina harbor adjacent to the campground. Few incidents were recorded in the campground loop or the tent only area. All of these violations are from official park reports. They included: one case of assault and intimidation; six thefts of personal property from camping vehicles, and boats on trailers parked next to camping vehicles; one citation for a dog being off a leash; four physical confrontations between campers; one case of spousal abuse; one sexual assault; one drug use violation; and eight citations for minor in possession of alcohol. In addition to these official violations, I also documented in my personal journal: 18 situations in which dog owners were warned to keep their pets on a leash; 27 incidents of visitors creating a noisy disturbance after 10:00 P.M.; 17 minor visitor confrontations over picnic tables and camping sites; three alcohol parties without minors being involved; three dog fights; one bicycle accident; and five incidents of abusive language from minors. All of these violations are prohibited by the Code of Federal Regulations 36(CFRs), which are administered by the National Park Service in areas under their jurisdiction.

Discussion

The breakdown of camping rules and norms in an area such as the overflow may lead to a breakdown of relations among the campers. This promotes rule violations, overcrowding, poor standards, and weakened social controls, arising from rapid turn over of the population. Once this has taken place, criminal activity becomes established as an enduring feature of the area (Davidson). In urban areas, poor or deteriorating environments have been correlated to higher rates of crime. Overcrowding in housing is considered to be related to a higher incidence of crime (Roncek). This too is a factor in the overflow transition area. It is always subject to overcrowding. The situation is such that campers will park their recreational vehicles directly in front of each other and even occasionally block the whole parking lot. This may be an important factor in the reoccurrence of crimes within this area.

Stark states that density is one aspect which characterizes high levels of deviance in urban areas. This is evidenced in this rural area also. "The greater the density of a neighborhood, the more that density is one aspect which characterizes high levels of deviance in urban areas. Stark's proposition one, "The greater the density of a neighborhood, the more association between those most and least predisposed to deviance," applies to the overflow area as well as to urban areas. In a dense area, such as the overflow, individuals prone to deviate are in close proximity to those unlikely to deviate. The peer group in areas of high density tends to be inclusive, the group which tends to deviate will dominate the latter. This tends to reconfirm the strong influence differential association may also have in situations such as these, providing the individuals are in close proximity for long enough periods of time.

Abeyie-Georges and Harries state that crime occurrence is more frequent in the central and interior areas of urban places. These areas are generally ones in which levels of activity are high and adjacent high-density residential areas are in poor condition. This condition of dilapidation relates to Stark's proposition number 17, which states, "Dilapidation is a social stigma for residents." The conditions of an urban area reflect the status of the residents. This is also true in the overflow area. The dilapidated condition of the overflow affects the temporary status of the resident. The conditions as compared to camping conditions elsewhere are indeed in very poor shape. The level of activity in this transition area is very high. Campers, boaters, sightseers and others are in constant flux through this area. Abeyie-Georges and

Harries further state that the quality of residential land use is related to crime occurrence. Crime occurrence is more frequent in deteriorating areas like the overflow campground. Different land use is related to specific offenses; differences in available targets; or potential victims are often noted as a function of the activities of an area. Do specific areas actually draw criminals to commit crimes? Stark writes, "Poor, dense, mixed-use neighborhoods have high transience rates". . .and transience reduces levels of community surveillance." The overflow area is the most run down area of the campground and the most transient. It is also utilized by a mixed group of campers (i.e., tents, RVs, people who sleep out on the ground, sleep in their cars, etc.). This type of mixed use and transiency draws criminal activity to the overflow area, the same as it draws deviant activity to urban areas.

In any transaction between people and their environment, they are either active toward the environment or they react to it (Abeyie-Georges and Harries). The transaction may be physical or cognitive, either tangible or symbolic. The campers may vandalize the place or go around and tell other campers that they are never coming back here because of the poor conditions.

Last summer, a group of people drove 300 miles to this campground. It was a place they had never been before. Someone told them it was a delightful family campground. They arrived late at night. It was a hot August night, and everyone was stacked in the overflow. The people in the group were not family members but friends; their tolerance for each other grew thin after a long trip and finding such crowded conditions. They started a fight with each other, this soon spread to their neighbor campers, over the rights to picnic tables. Later that night the kids from this group stole a lantern from the neighbors on the other side. When questioned, they responded, "It was just laying there, nobody would care if we took it." This illustrates a breakdown of social control and a reaction to the poor conditions within the overflow transition area.

Davidson states that crime rates revolve around the development of neighborhood norms, in this case campground norms, related to criminality. It involves the degree of tolerance an individual expresses towards a particular crime or the tolerance towards an offenders' behavior with a ranger. Attitudes about crime are the key factors in tolerance of criminal behavior. Whether this tolerance for criminal activity is a result of the social disorganization of the zone in transition or of a general urban attitude, I can not say from the limited observations of this one campground.

Social disorganization is severely criticized for only being applicable to the poor and lower socioeconomic status. In this model of social disorganization, the theory applies to the upper and middle classes also. All classes of individuals inhabit this area. The loop area and the tent area also accommodate all classes of individuals. These areas do not experience the high crime rate which occurs in the overflow area. Some individuals react in a negative manner when they are confronted with rapid change and new emergent norms. This is evidenced by the overflow's high rate of deviance.

Felson and Cohen (1980) state that everyday activities may be responsible for high crime rates in transitory areas. They argue that everyday activities of individuals and families are the keys to understanding why crime rates are so high in our society. This may also explain the extremely high rates of crime in this overflow area of the campground. Felson and Cohen take the approach that increased crime is caused by more dual careers for couples, this places more people outside of the home at different hours; more people live by themselves in independent households; the extension of shopping hours into the night; more individuals eating outside their homes; and so on. These activities, say Felson and Cohen, bring together potential targets and offenders. The normal everyday activities of today's society place people at higher risk for crime. Hindelang et al. (1978) state that certain life-styles lead to an increase of movement among individuals and through their activities, this exposes individuals to a greater level of risk with potential offenders.

This same routine activity approach can also apply to the crime problem in the overflow. The campground is home to many anglers. As a rule these people are usually absent from camp early in the morning and after dark in the evening. This type of activity is participated in because the fish are biting, and they bite early and late on this lake. This absence from camp presents an excellent opportunity for a potential offender to help themselves to anything that happens to be left in the open. During the daylight hours, the campers who enjoy water sports are also out of the area, another prime opportunity. While at the campground, because of the unusual hours they keep, camper/anglers tend to eat their evening meal later than they would if they were at home, this places them in the company with the party crowd. The party crowd is used to late hours and they are usually younger and heavier users of alcohol and drugs. The two groups are not compatible. The camper/anglers get up early to go fishing, while the camper/party person, sleeps late and stays up into the wee hours of the night. This particular combination of activities provokes a few conflicts in the campground. The routine activity approach combined with social disorganization accounts for the increased crime in the overflow. The routine activity approach should also account for some deviant activity within the loop and the tent only area, but very little deviant activity occurs there. I attribute this to the fact that these areas are very structured, there are rules and the sites are carefully delineated and less dense. There is little room for disorganization in these other areas.

CONCLUSIONS

What can be done to solve this problem in the overflow area? The first and most obvious solution would be to eliminate the overflow. This solution has been suggested to the Park Service and the suggestion was turned down. The National Park Service maintains that it must provide as many facilities to the public as is physically possible. The Park Service has a new campground planned, but budgetary restraints prevent the development at the present time. This situation will have to be tolerated until the new campground is built.

Oscar Newman's theory of defensible space states that certain designs in urban housing can affect the probability of various type of criminal acts. Certain types of environmental behavioral information is sought by the criminal before selecting a target (Brantingham and Brantingham). The amount of privacy available to the perspective target influences the possibility of whether the crime will be committed. If the potential target is perceived to be in public space the criminal will hesitate less in making the decision to strike. A camper in the overflow area may be viewed as more publicly accessible than a camper in the loop, which has limited access. Detectability is another factor. In the overflow area people pull in at all hours of the day and night, therefore, a person would be less detectable, because this is a common occurrence. In the loop an intruder would attract the attention of another camper. Social climate is the last factor mentioned by Newman. It is the extent to which people exhibit shared concern for an area and for the type of behavior permitted by strangers. In the loop it would be inappropriate for strangers to roam at night and to make loud noises. In the overflow this is constantly happening.

People who commit crime try to avoid being seen. Ranger patrol is a deterrent, although due to the lack of numbers ranger patrol, is not totally effective. The available evidence shows that the chances that witnesses will see a crime being committed are very small (Brantingham and Brantingham, 1980). First, people frequently fail to notice a crime taking place. Second, even if a person does witness a crime, he/she may interpret it to be something else. Third, eyewitnesses are reluctant to challenge offenders or to become involved in an incident. Fourth, people fail to call a ranger because they think it is a minor offense and that it would be too late by the time a ranger arrived. They may also be too embarrassed to report some crimes. Finally, there is not much risk at being positively identified by a witness when an offender is seen again. Even with all of this in mind offenders still avoid being seen when committing a crime.

Therefore, it is suggested that the National Park Service limit accessibility to the overflow area during the nighttime hours. Increase the lighting in this area to increase detectability and post the campground rules and regulations where they are easily accessed by the campers in the overflow area.

References

Abeyie-Georges, D.E. and K. D. Harries (eds.) *Crime: A Spatial Perspective* (New York: Columbia University Press) 1980.

Brantingham, P.J. and P.L. Brantingham (eds.), Environmental Criminology (Beverly Hills CA: Sage Publishing) 1980.

Burgess, E.W. and R.E. Parks and M. McKenzie (eds.)*The City* (Chicago: University of Chicago Press) 1925.

Bursik, R.J. Jr., "Urban Dynamics and Ecological Studies of Delinquency". *Social Forces,* 63:2. 393-410, 1984.

Bursik, R.J. Jr., "Social Disorganization and Theories of Crime and Delinquency: Problems and Prospects," *Criminology,* 26:4. 519-551, 1988.

Davidson, R.N., *Crime and Environment* (London: Croom Helm) 1981.

Faris, R. E. and H.W. Dunham, "Natural Area of the City." *Theories of Deviance* (Itasca, IL: Peacock Publishers) 50-58, 1985.

Felson, M. and L.E. Cohen, "Human Ecology and Crime: A Routine Activity Approach," *Human Ecology* , 8: 389-406, 1980.

Felson, M., "Linking Criminal Choices, Routine Activities, Informal Control and Criminal Outcomes," *The Reasoning Criminal.* (New York: Springer-Verlag)pp. 119-128, 1986.

Gibbons, D.C., *The Criminological Enterprise* (Engelwood Cliffs NJ: Prentice Hall) 44-45, 1979.

Hindelang, M.J., M.R. Gottfredson, and J. Garofalo,*Victims of Personal Crime: An Empirical Foundation for a Theory of Personal Victimization.* Cambridge, MA: Ballinger, 1978.

Kornhauser, R.R., *Social Sources of Delinquency,* Chicago: University of Chicago Press, 1978.

National Park Service, *Visitation Figures and Ranger Reports*, 1992.

Roncek, D.W., "Density and Crime: A Methodological Critique." *American Behavioral Scientist:* 18. 843-860, 1975.

Shaw, C.R. and H. McKay, *Juvenile Delinquency and Urban Areas*. Chicago: University of Chicago Press, 1942.

Stark, R.,"Deviant Places: A Theory of the Ecology of Crime," *Criminology* 25:4. 893-909, 1987.

Thomas, W.I. and F. Znaniecki, "The Polish Peasant in Europe and America," *Theories of Deviance* (Itasca, Il: Peacock Publishers) pp.44-46, 1985.

CHAPTER *12*

ILLEGAL DRUGS AND OUR NATIONAL PARKS

H
ow many people would walk down the street after dark in the Watts area of Los Angeles with a wad of cash in their fist? How many backpackers and other backcountry visitors never give a second thought to hiking their favorite wilderness trails? Most visitors to the national park backcountry areas never think about the violence and danger that exists in these areas. I do not mean danger from wild animals or from falling off cliffs. I am speaking about the danger from illegal marijuana growers and other individuals who manufacture drugs in our national parks. Drugs were reported to be a major violation in 38 percent of the parks in which I conducted ranger interviews.

ILLEGAL DRUG PRODUCTION

In 1991, the National Park Service compiled the following statistics. Rangers and other law enforcement officers:

- Made 1,046 drug-related arrests

- Seized over $202 million worth of marijuana

- Confiscated 76 weapons and seven traps

- Destroyed 280,389 marijuana plants (NPS, 1991) (This is only a small portion of the actual marijuana which is being produced in our parks.)

Why are park lands being used to grow and manufacture drugs? Many drug labs are moved to remote locations in the backcountry because they exude a strong odor when they are producing drugs. The backcountry offers the producer and grower some added protections. If the grower's crop is discovered by law enforcement rangers, all the grower loses is his crop. If the marijuana were found growing on private land, then everything the individual owned would be subject to forfeiture, according to the drug enforcement laws of the United States. This type of enterprise poses an extreme danger to the backcountry user because the visitor is usually unaware of the danger posed by these growers until it is too late.

Some of the national parks which have been affected by drug manufacture and marijuana production are in Arizona, California, Nevada, Maine, Utah, Tennessee, and Minnesota. This movement onto park lands has caused the National Park Service to become extremely concerned for the safety of its visitors. The National Park Service received 1.7 million dollars in 1991 to fight the drug problem in the parks (Dwyer, et al.). The park service has begun to urge their visitors to use the backcountry with caution. There have been some visitors who have been harassed and threatened with bodily harm if they approach a marijuana plot too closely. Some "pot growers" employ the use of dogs, booby traps and alarm systems to protect their patches of "pot." These individuals also impact the environment.

── Real Life Situation ──────

Dale Antonich of Lake Mead National Recreation Area reports a meth lab, which they found aboard a houseboat on Lake Mead. The producers were apprehended by National Park Service rangers. During the "bust," the producers dumped the glassware and the hazardous chemical materials, such as sulfuric acid and ether, used to make the drugs into the lake. This caused an extreme hazardous condition. The chemicals were spilled into the water where they disseminated. All the NPS can do now is to pull the containers out of the water. These drug manufacturers do not care what happens to the environment as long as they make a profit.

The National Park Service has established a program aimed at ridding the park backcountry of marijuana growers and drug labs. It consists of four parts:

1) Detection (e.g., overflights, rewards for information leading to the arrest and conviction of growers)

2) Visitor safety and public awareness, through the media, pamphlets, individual contacts, news releases, and interpretive programs

3) Employee safety (i.e., training and instruction)

4) Law enforcement (including patrol, prevention, eradication, and the arrest of growers)

WAR ON DRUGS IN OUR PARKS

The "war on drugs" has been carried into the parks. Our resources and visitors must be protected.

Detection and enforcement sometimes go hand-in-hand in park operations. Many national parks utilize the services of undercover rangers. These rangers disguise themselves as potential buyers or pushers and attempt to catch the dealer in the act. Undercover operations exist in most of our large national parks, such as Yosemite, Yellowstone, Lake Mead, Glacier, and Glen Canyon. These operations usually target the user because targeting the dealer is not productive. The demand for the drug will still exist, and someone else will soon take the dealer's place. The better alternative is to target the user. This approach will serve as a deterrent for others who would buy and use the drugs in the parks.

Undercover rangers are often in the field at Lake Mead National Recreation Area. This NPS area does the most undercover work, according to Chief Ranger Dale Antonich. It seems that there are many clandestine drug labs which operate in the desolate backcountry of Lake Mead. There are many airstrips serving these labs. They also have floatplane landings on the lake to pickup and deliver illegal substances. The park utilizes one undercover vessel and four undercover patrol vehicles. These are painted and outfitted so the rangers can drive them right up in the middle of a crowd, and they fit right in. Antonich states that in 1992, they had one ranger assigned to full-time undercover operations. This means that the ranger is out of uniform and "dirty" all the time. The park hires six seasonals for the summer season. According to the chief ranger, once these seasonals are working, he puts six permanent rangers into undercover work. They use trucks as their vehicles, and they do a lot of drug buying. They make many drug busts that way. The trucks are fitted to the profile of the local crowd and so is the undercover ranger. This use of undercover rangers for targeting drug users is an excellent public relations tool. The publicity of many arrests in a park for drug use signals the public that the park is serious about curtailing and eliminating the sale and use of drugs (Dwyer, et al.).

A great deal of care must be exercised in the patrol of today's park areas. The situation has changed from the carefree days of the 40s and 50s. What appears to be a group of young people camping in an area, may turn out to be a meth lab or something worse.

— Real Life Situation —————————————

A young, seasonal ranger had just radioed into the park's dispatcher that he would be returning to the ranger station when he observed a set of vehicle tracks in the desert sand. These tracks went up a two track path into a group of rock outcroppings. The ranger parked his patrol vehicle and followed the tracks on foot, because the use of vehicles off established roads is prohibited. He happened upon a camp that appeared to be a group of young people in an area that was not designated for camping. Upon approaching the area, he noticed that there were five vehicles parked in a box canyon. He observed a generator and some other miscellaneous camping equipment. The ranger thought that this was just another illegal camp. He used tunnel vision. This is what he expected it to be; however, it was not what it was. It was a full blown meth lab, operated by members of the "Hells Angels" biker gang. The ranger who found this lab had the foresight to take the keys out of the vehicles as he approached the site to prevent the "campers" from attempting to leave the area until each one could be cited. The only reason this ranger escaped from this situation with his life is because the bikers made a mistake too.

The bikers had posted lookouts on the ridge, and they monitored all of the law enforcement frequencies which were used by the NPS, the BLM, and local sheriffs' departments. They heard the ranger radio his dispatcher and say he was on his way back to the ranger station. They also knew that this ranger was the only law enforcement officer in the area at that time. The "meth" producers thought that they had covered their tracks and had no idea that this ranger would spot them. One vehicle used by the biker group was able to escape the area, but on the way out of the canyon, the occupants managed to hide their production of "speed" pills.

The ranger beat a hasty retreat and radioed for backup when he realized that this was no illegal camp but a "meth" lab. In the time between the initial contact and the time backup officers arrived, the "meth" lab people buried their chemicals and other equipment, and they threw bottles of ether and sulfuric acid into holes in the ground. The chemicals soaked into the dry desert soil. The area was eventually surrounded by rangers and the culprits were apprehended, but not before a million dollars worth of damage was done to the fragile desert ecosystem. The drugs which were hidden by the vehicle that initially escaped were also found a short distance from the scene. The National Park Service won convictions in that case, but the damage from the dumping of all those chemicals poses a cleanup problem for the park to this day.

The lesson to be learned from this incident is to think ahead. Think of "what if" questions. Approach areas that appear to be "just another illegal campsite" as something more until it proves to be otherwise. Don't take chances, call in suspicious activities, before approaching. This ranger was lucky, others who choose to take similar actions may not be quite so fortunate. Tunnel vision is dangerous. Look at the whole picture. Ask yourself what is wrong with a particular scene. Tunnel vision has killed more law enforcement officers than any other form of carelessness.

— Real Life Situation ————————————————

Two conservation officers were killed in Idaho by Claude Dallas because of their tunnel vision. The officers approached Dallas's camp with one thing in mind. They knew Dallas was a poacher, and they wanted enough evidence to convict him. They were busy looking at the illegally poached animals and animal hides around Dallas's camp, so they did not notice Dallas when he went for his weapon. Both conservation officers were shot and then brutally murdered with a shot to their heads. Their deaths were the direct result of their own tunnel vision. Look at the whole picture and watch your suspect!

Marijuana growing occurs in many backcountry areas of our National Park System. Acadia National Park reported a dozen marijuana plantations within its borders over the past ten years. Chief Ranger Norm Dodge said that the park received assistance from the National Guard. According to Dodge, they sent in some jungle fighters in order to check the swamps in the park for marijuana plantations, and they found a dozen sites. The operation seemed to work; the next couple of years marijuana patches disappeared. Dodge says that most of the growing is done by the local residents. The word gets around that the rangers are looking for marijuana plantations, then the "dope" dries up. If the pressure is let up, the "potgrowers" move back in. Dodge and his rangers do not intend to "let up" on the pressure. Bruce Mckeeman of Voyageur National Park recalls another incident with marijuana growers when he worked in Hawaii at Hawaii Volcanoes National Park.

— Real Life Situation ——————————

The two years that I was in Hawaii we were faced with a very critical issue. Hawaii, from a climatological standpoint, has some very good growing seasons. The marijuana growers had pretty much taken over the backcountry in Hawaii Volcanoes National Park to the point where resource crews were refusing to do any resource management work in the backcountry. We chose to reclaim the backcountry, and it was very easy for us because this park has definite boundaries. It was much more difficult for a small police department to police a whole island. We went into a stakeout post, and we would fly the park with a helicopter to locate the plots. Whenever we located a plot, we would set up stakeouts. We would be in there for three to seven days watching the crop, waiting for people to come in and manipulate, fertilize and tend their crops. At that point we would arrest them for production and intent to distribute, felony charges. We arrested 26 people for felony cultivation the first year. We spent the next year in federal court in Honolulu getting 26 convictions; we did not lose a case. Some plead out, some went to trial, but we did convict all of them one way or another. It was pretty difficult because the defendants brought pretrial motions that a photograph of a person tending a crop was not good enough. But we coupled it with fact, multiple observations, and personal knowledge. They were rock solid cases.

Marijuana cases are made by rangers in most of our national parks. These cases may consist of growers or of just making busts of users. It is important to keep up the fight to prevent our park backcountry from becoming havens for "pot growers" and drug manufacturers. All of our California national parks have been, or are currently, impacted from marijuana production. Whiskey Town National Recreation Area reports drug use and production as an important violation as does Yosemite National Park. Ranger Chris Cruz reports many cases of marijuana production occurring in isolated backcountry areas within Yosemite National Park. In one case, several hundred plants were destroyed and several individuals were arrested and convicted.

Drug Use in Our Parks

Chief Ranger Larry Clark from Glen Canyon National Recreation Area complains about the usage of drugs on the beaches of his NRA. "Lone Rock Beach, four or five years ago, was rated one of the top 10 beaches in the United States by Playboy. They go out there and party. That is one of our problems—alcohol. There are a lot of injuries because people are misusing alcohol or drugs. Drugs would probably be a big item on the lake if we had a way to approach handling it, because I think we have a lot of recreational use of drugs. They bring it and use it like alcohol. A lot of our population comes out of California and everybody brings their alcohol. Ninety-five percent of the people here have alcohol, and there is a good   percentage that are recreational drug users. One of my biggest problems is when we have boating violations that result in property damage and injury. We have a number of accidents that result from slips and falls in the water and people drown. We have people who dive off of high cliffs and houseboats and break their necks; we have a large number of those who die. Frequently, they involve alcohol.

Alcohol is the most commonly abused drug in the United States. This is in evidence in all of our national parks. Most crimes are alcohol or drug related. The next case concerns an individual under the influence of a controlled substance in one of our most peaceful national parks, Isle Royale. The incident is related by Chief Ranger Stuart L. Kroll:

—— Real Life Situation ————————

We had gotten word from a visitor that there was a deranged individual (we get this kind of thing all the time) on the island that was acting suspicious. We alerted the park people; it was a cold dreary night in September. A person raced into Rock Harbor saying there is a crazy man down at Three-mile Campground.

We got down there and, sure enough, here is this guy stuffing money into bird's nests and woodpecker holes. So we questioned him, and the guy pulled a knife on us. A scuffle took place, and the man was arrested and brought back to Rock Harbor. As we were questioning him at the visitor's center, we left the weapon nearby. The suspect pulled out the knife and tried to stab the desk clerk. He missed and stabbed the desk. This occurred around 11:00 at night. We didn't have any place to incarcerate people, so we had to sit up all night with the character, fly him off in handcuffs and strait-jacket another 110 miles to the magistrate to do his thing, and then put him in jail. We later discovered that the man had tried to kill his parents the week before. We also found out he had tried to kill somebody else in his family a week before that. I think, to this day, he is still incarcerated in some mental institution.

We don't [typically] have that kind of thing here. The funny thing is that we had a fire control aide who noticed that the knife point was broken off. The incident occurred so late at night that we had forgotten to tag it as a piece of evidence. He took that knife and ground it right down to make it brand new again. The FBI agent said that it was a good thing that we didn't have to go to court.

There are many lessons to be learned from this case. One, of course, is not to leave evidence in an unlocked area. Another is to label evidence. Suspects must always be carefully handled and treated as a threat. Rangers must never let up their guard, even after the individual appears to be under control.

Chief Ranger Larry Van Slyke reports that drugs of all kinds are a problem in Zion. He further states that the Utah State Patrol officers on Interstate 15 and Interstate 70, which are almost adjacent to Zion, made more drug busts on the highways than did the states of Colorado, Arizona, Montana, and Idaho combined. According to Van Slyke, the state patrol officers are becoming so good at picking out these drug vehicles that people are getting "spooked." This is causing the large shipments of drugs to be funneled down the backroads through Zion National Park and Grand Canyon National Park.

Zion had a total of twenty drug busts in 1992. In one case, rangers confiscated marijuana, cocaine, methadone, mushrooms, and $2000 in cash. The two individuals who were arrested had long histories in trafficking drugs. Their car was seized along with the cash. These individuals were selling the drugs in Zion's campgrounds.

Many problems exist in the national parks which have to be solved by law enforcement park rangers. Keeping drugs, drug dealers, producers, and users out is just one of the things rangers must face. The war on drugs may not be won, but it is the duty of rangers to be sure that these substances do not impair the preservation or use and enjoyment of our park backcountry by the citizens of the United States. The blight of drug use in our parks is a constant threat to visitor safety. Drug arrests are being made in parks where a few short years ago, they were unheard of. All of these problems are symptomatic of our society. The war on drugs must be fought on all lines, beginning with the producer and ending with the user. If education is not successful, then we will move up the ladder of enforcement until the problem is solved.

References

Dwyer, W., D. Murrell, B. Wages and J. Lisco, "Drug Enforcement in Parks: Targeting the User" *Parks and Recreation*, pps.56-61, Feb. 1991.

National Park Service, Dept. of the Interior, Washington D.C., 1991.

CHAPTER *13*

RANGER PROTECTION

The life of a ranger is exciting, but typically not too dangerous. What must be remembered, however, is that law enforcement rangers are sworn federal officers. They do face the same dangers as all other law enforcement officers. Each year rangers are assaulted, shot at, and sometimes killed in the line of duty. In the summer of 1993, a ranger was shot three times in Yosemite National Park by an unknown gunman. Bob McGhee, a ranger at the Gulf Islands National Seashore, was gunned down and killed by two escaped convicts in 1990. Rangers must be prepared at all times to meet the challenge of today's criminal element.

PROTECT YOURSELF

A firearms instructor once told me that the only way to train is with the idea that it will help you go home to your family every night. The parks now provide body armor for their rangers. If it is available, wear it. I admit that backcountry use of body armor is difficult, but at least take it with you. If you don't take it, then it can't do you a bit of good. Many rangers who work the backcountry areas of our national parks even object to carrying a firearm while on backcountry patrol. The comment most often heard is "Nothing happens in the backcountry, I'll just leave it home this time." Chief Ranger Larry Van Slyke relates this particular incident when he left his weapon home. Larry said that you cannot assume that just because you are in the backcountry you won't run into many types of situations. One incident that he remembered was a mistake he made shortly after he arrived at Grand Canyon.

—— Real Life Situation ——

Larry was getting ready to hike down into the canyon. He thought to himself, "I am just going down to Phantom Ranch. I do not need my gun and handcuffs." Larry left them at home that day. He arrived at the ranch, and he wasn't there more than 15 minutes when he received a call from a trail crew, half way up the Kaibab Trail that there was a person there who was acting very peculiar. The person was totally irrational and definitely a dangerous threat to himself and to others. Larry says,"It was sort of embarrassing for me, because I had to call for a helicopter in order to be flown up there. I also had to ask the ranger who flew it to bring some restraining devices with him. I tried to ask in a very subtle manner, but I still came off looking very unprepared." The ranger brought the appropriate equipment to Larry, then they both contacted the man. He was a young person in his early twenties who didn't know where he was or who he was. From the condition of his eyes, Larry suspected that the individual was high on mushrooms. Still Larry felt very compassionate toward the young man, he seemed like a real lost soul. They placed him in the chopper, handcuffed him, and put a restricting band around his upper arms to keep him secure in the helicopter. Larry sat in the rear with the man. As the chopper climbed to two thousand feet above the Colorado River, the man unbuckled his seatbelt, reached over and opened the door intending to jump. With all the movement in the rear, the pilot and other ranger became pretty excited. Larry grabbed the guy's helmet and pulled him back into the chopper. The rangers thought that they were dealing with a medical emergency, and it turned out to be a suicidal individual. "The person could have easily decided to take everyone with him, and I was up there with no weapon," Larry said.

SUICIDE ATTEMPTS

Many of the national parks are places in which people wish to use as sites for their deaths. According to Chuck Sypher, the Grand Canyon National Park is the park most chosen for suicide attempts. Individuals drive their vehicles off of overlooks into the Canyon, they jump out of sight-seeing helicopters, and, occasionally, they take their would-be rescuers with them. Who would those would-be rescuers be? The law enforcement park ranger. There are a few things a ranger should be aware of when dealing with a person with suicidal tendencies.

If you encounter such a situation, your job is to keep the person from killing himself or from killing innocent people. If your life or someone else's is threatened, the suicidal person's life may have to be taken. The role of a ranger is not to treat the mental illness of the person but to aid in the immediate crisis. Mental health officials can take care of the treatment of the individual later on. If the suicide victim is despondent, listen to him/her, keep him/her occupied. These people are in real pain, and if you listen, it may alleviate the pain, and you may be able to diffuse the situation safely. There is no emergency more emotionally draining for the ranger than a suicide attempt.

Remember to use the utmost safety precautions at all times. Use a low, confident voice when speaking to the person. Let the person ventilate his or her anger or anxiety. If you think the person is really contemplating suicide, ask the question, "Are you going to kill yourself?" If you get an affirmative reply, then you must consider how the person plans on doing it. Did they already take pills, poison or drugs? In Grand Canyon, Zion, and Yosemite, it is usually the "jump." Suicide victims usually wish to draw attention to their final act. This gives the ranger an opportunity to save a life, although this may not always be the case. At times, the ranger is just left with the grisly duty of cleaning up the remains.

— Real Life Situations ————————

The rangers of Coulee Dam National Recreation Area searched in vain for one drowning victim while they received a radio call concerning a suicide victim's body which was found a couple of miles away. The person had jumped off the bridge in Trail, British Columbia, and his body floated downstream into the NRA. Ranger Gig LeBret was responsible for picking this poor bloated body out of the lake and returning it to the Canadian authorities. This is the most distasteful job a ranger must perform. The ranger must deal with many people in many capacities and must be prepared for the worst.

Coulee Dam National Recreation Area, South District Ranger, Gil Goodrich related this incident to me a few years ago.

While Goodrich was a ranger at Grand Canyon he was faced with a hostage situation. A deranged concession employee took a hostage by knifepoint and threatened to kill the hostage. This occurred in a park hotel's employee dormitory. Goodrich was present at the time the hostage was taken. He could have chosen to shoot the individual immediately, since the opportunity did present itself; however, Goodrich chose not to. He and other rangers were able to convince the deranged individual to release his hostage and to give himself up.

This is the kind of work our National Park Service rangers are called upon to perform. Firearms are necessary, but they should be used only when there is no other choice. Goodrich believed, and rightly so, that there was another choice. Use your weapon if it will save a life that would otherwise be needlessly taken.

For years, rangers have been told by various superintendents that they should not display their defensive equipment because the visitor might be offended. I decided to see if this really was the case. Were park visitors really upset because law enforcement rangers wore defensive equipment? All the rangers I interviewed, with the exception of one backcountry ranger in North Cascades National Park, told me that the visitor was not upset because they carried firearms. In fact, they felt the visitors actually felt safer because the rangers were armed. Ranger Kelly Bush of North Cascade National Park had this comment concerning firearms:

> Visitors approach her and say, "What's going on, why are you wearing a gun? Is there a lot of crime up here?" Most all people were offended by it, people came up here to experience wilderness and solitude and the last thing they want to see is something that reminds them of all the crime they left the city to get away from. The last thing, to be honest with you, that I want to pack around is ten pounds of law enforcement gear for a situation that may happen once in 28 years. I can only remember a couple of arrests that we ever made at the park, and they were at trailheads. So the couple of us that are faced with wilderness patrol are always faced with hauling all this law enforcement gear with us. We only carry what we need to carry. We do mostly resource protection. It is the way for me not to gain compliance by walking into a situation and being real authoritative, in my uniform and gun. In whatever situation you go into, the more credibility you have, the more compliance you will get. We make these decisions, sometimes we carry them, sometimes we carry them in a pack. We use our best judgement.

Chief Ranger Larry L. Hakel of Shenandoah National Park disagrees with Ranger Bush. He states, "Law-abiding visitors have no problem with rangers carrying guns. Violators are upset and feel threatened." Thirty other rangers and chief rangers echoed his statements. As far as can be ascertained, there are no studies of visitor attitudes concerning rangers and firearms. It would be interesting to research their attitudes and concerns.

Parks, in which a great deal of backcountry exists, allow their rangers to carry their weapons in specially-designed fanny packs, which allow fast access to the weapon. But even in these parks, the rangers are cautioned to have their defensive weapons readily available. Chief Ranger Dale Antonich was quite emphatic concerning the carrying and use of defensive weapons by the rangers under his command. He put it this way:

> I have worked at parks where the administration was against firearms. I worked at the Grand Canyon, Santa Monica Mountains, Golden Gate, Grand Tetons, and Death Valley, and I have never heard a visitor complain about a ranger wearing a weapon. As a chief ranger, I have never received a complaint, and that's been seven years as a chief ranger. I was an assistant chief ranger for five years and never received a complaint. As a law enforcement specialist at the Grand Tetons, I never received a complaint. I've had rangers request to carry their firearms in backpacks. They just did not accept the fact that law enforcement happened in the backcountry. At Grand Tetons, maybe it doesn't happen as often, but they still get incidents. When I arrived there, carrying a gun in a pack was an option, when I left, it was not an option. After I left, it became an option again. Its a management mindset, I don't think the public cares one iota whether you're armed or not.
>
> I was in the Santa Monica Mountains and in the San Francisco Bay Area and remember the Hillside strangler and all of that. Those people would say, "It's nice to see you back here." They would see your gun; they knew who you were and what you were doing.

Chief Ranger Bob Powell, from Theodore Roosevelt National Park, says that visitors actually feel safer when rangers are armed. Theodore Roosevelt National Park is renown for its lack of crime. The advice from all these rangers is be prepared and carry your defensive equipment. Hopefully it will never be needed, but as my friend John Kauppunen always said, "Be sure you go home after work."

I believe that many assaults and ranger shootings can be avoided with the proper training and adequate knowledge. Always have your firearm available and easily accessible. Practice the various defensive tactics available to all law enforcement officers. Know how to defend yourself against knife attacks. The knowledge of chemical weapons can save a life. Pepper spray, OC-10, is a safe effective defensive weapon which is totally harmless. It burns the eyes and skin, but the effects usually are short lived. I recommend it over the collapsible baton and other club type weapons. If the spray is taken away from the officer, it cannot cause death or disfigurement. It is also easy to carry into the backcountry. It can be kept in a pack, fannypack, or in a pocket, as well as on your defensive equipment belt. Soft body armor is also good insurance for the law enforcement ranger. This, however, is not always a feasible option. Body armor is often difficult, if not impossible, to wear while hiking a mountain trail or while operating a boat in 100 degree heat. The soft body armor manufacturers have come a long way since its conception a few years ago. Someday it may be as light as a uniform shirt. When possible, wear it. Get into the habit of putting it on. Even if you only wear it while working at night, it cuts down your risk considerably. Finally, the use of two-man patrols and the use of backup will prevent many more ranger assaults. If there is a possibility of becoming fatally injured and you have a choice of waiting for a backup ranger, then wait!

In answer to all of the headquarter personnel who object to rangers wearing guns, I would like to make this reply. The presence of a weapon is a deterrent to ranger assault. Rangers will still be shot at, but, in most cases, the assailant will think twice about shooting at an armed ranger. I suggest all rangers become familiar with their firearms, practice, and always take them on patrol.

Many courses are available in defensive tactics and in officer survival. I recommend that all of you take some additional courses in these subjects. The more training you have, the better you will be able to cope with these types of situations.

References

Harmon, L., "How to Make Park Law Enforcement Work for You," *Parks and Recreation*, pp.20-21, Dec.1979.

National Mental Health Association, *Aiding People in Conflict*, Alexandria, VA.,1988.

CHAPTER 14

A DAY IN THE LIFE OF A
NATIONAL PARK SERVICE RANGER

W hat's it like to be a park ranger? This is an often asked question. I have heard it many times. Answering this question may give prospective rangers insight into the duties they will face.

It was another typically hot morning on Lake Roosevelt, which is what makes up the majority of the Coulee Dam National Recreation Area. Ranger "Luke" began the first day of his work week. He quickly ran through in his mind, the things which needed to be accomplished this day. He needed to check the campgrounds at Keller Ferry and Jones Bay. The area at Jones Bay, which had been impacted by ORVs the previous year, had to be photographed. The lifeguard on duty at Keller Ferry must be briefed. The area of lake between Keller Ferry and Lincoln Mill, a distance of 40 miles round trip, must be patrolled by boat. He was to meet the park's resource management specialist at Jones Bay at 11:00 A.M. A busy day for one ranger, but all in a days work.

The campground patrol at Keller Ferry is conducted on foot. Luke believes that this is the best method to make contact with the visitor. Visitors react in a negative manner if the only rangers they encounter are always in a patrol vehicle. His patrol reveals an illegal catch of fish and a couple of marijuana cigarettes. Luke observed the campers carrying filleted fish to their camper. He stopped them to inform them that filleting fish was only allowed if they were to be eaten immediately. Fish prepared in this manner for transportation are considered to be mutilated. This is a violation of Washington state law. The violators acted very nervous. Luke asked if they had more fish in their freezer. They replied, "It's none of your business, get a warrant." Luke said, "I don't need a warrant, if you have illegal fish, then I can look." In the process of looking, Luke found two unsmoked marijuana cigarettes on the table, in plain view. He seized the evidence and cited the violators. They then left the area. The violation would have gone unnoticed if the patrol was conducted from a vehicle.

The lifeguard is briefed for the days work, and Luke heads out to his other campgrounds. After fueling up the patrol rig, a 1987 Jeep Cherokee, Luke heads for Jones Bay and a meeting with the Resource Management Specialist. The meeting was established to look over an area which was severely impacted by off-road vehicles the year before. The case is finally going to court and the damages need to be reassessed and photographs need to be taken. While taking the photographs at Jones Bay, Luke receives a radio message that there has been a fire sighted on Lake Roosevelt near Sterling Point.

The message was given to Luke by ranger Russ Walker of another subdistrict. Luke works on the Spring Canyon Subdistrict. Walker does not know the exact location of the fire. Luke responds to the information by telling the resource specialist that he will have to continue the photography session at another time. He gets into the Jeep and drives off to the fire. On the way back to the marina at Keller Ferry, Luke is in contact with his district ranger and second line supervisor, Gil Goodrich. Goodrich gives Luke the crew boss responsibilities for fighting the fire and asks how many firefighters will be needed. Luke carefully replies, "Send a crew of five, and if we need more help, I'll contact you at the fire."

The fastest way to the location where the fire was spotted is by boat. The patrol boat is fully equipped with firefighting gear. It is a 1989 Boston Whaler with a 150 hp Evinrude outboard motor. Luke is ready to go at approximately 12:15 P.M. He skillfully operates the vessel downstream at 45 miles per hour. When Luke arrives at the site of the reported fire, he is met by Walker and two other National Park Service employees, Tom Lutyens and Carl Sanders. Not knowing the exact location of the fire, Luke sent another employee by land with a pumper truck. This was a futile effort, however, because the fire was located on the reservation side of the lake and could not be reached by land. This other employee returned to the ranger station.

Since the fire was located on an Indian reservation, Luke radioed the district ranger and requested instructions. Goodrich called the tribal dispatch and then informed Luke to extinguish the fire and then wait for the tribal firefighters to arrive before leaving the scene. Luke agreed. The crew, headed by ranger Luke, climbed the 1,000 foot slope up to the site of the fire. A lone ponderosa pine was burning. It was the victim of an isolated lightning strike. Luke's crew soon had the fire out. They awaited the arrival of an Indian fire crew and turned the mop up operations over to them. Luke and his crew, tired and dirty after fighting this fire for five hours, returned to their boats. Walker, Lutyens, and Sanders returned up stream to their duty station, and Luke returned to the Keller Ferry Marina, where he moored his vessel.

Upon return, he was notified that a local resident had suffered a fatal heart attack. Luke is the closest trained first aid person, and he responds to the situation. Sadly, the victim is an elderly woman, and it is too late. She has been dead for many hours. Luke helps the family by contacting the coroner's office and the local mortuary. Luke is depended upon by the local community for these types of services. He is looked upon as a friend, even though animosity exists between the National Park Service and the local residents.

The day is not over yet. Luke returns to his cabin near the Fort Spokane Ranger Station, with the intention to visit a campfire talk which his wife, Nora, is giving that evening. He is late and doesn't have time to change out of his uniform, so he goes in uniform. Luke isn't at the campfire program for more than 10 minutes when he must take care of a situation involving the illegal cutting of a tree.

It seems that three individuals cut down a tree for firewood. The cutting of trees in a national park is prohibited. Luke radios for assistance, because this is another ranger's jurisdiction. Walker soon arrives, and the two of them approach the individuals in campsite 53 at the Fort Spokane campground. Walker and Luke cite the individuals for destroying park vegetation. The two rangers then leave the scene.

Luke returns to the program being conducted by his wife. Again a frantic individual interrupts Luke's enjoyment of the program. "They are fighting in campsite 53," yells an elderly woman. Luke runs in the direction of campsite 53. He finds the three individuals he and Walker cited rolling on the ground, punching and kicking each other. Luke separates the individuals and tries to sort out the situation. The three were arguing over who was at fault in the tree incident. The situation cannot be allowed to continue. Luke radios Walker, and the rangers make their first arrest of the day. The individuals are transported to the district office, where Luke contacts the U.S. attorney's office. The U.S. attorney tells them to bring them in and lock them up. It's a long trip to the federally approved facility in Spokane, Washington, but Luke and Walker make the trip. They finally get their charges locked up. They both return to Fort Spokane about 6:00 A.M. the next morning, almost in time to begin a new day.

All days in the life of a national park ranger are not quite as hectic as this one , but a ranger is expected to have the stamina to survive an occasional day such as this.

Chapter 15

Looking Forward

A Ranger Is?

The criminal acts and violations which occur on a steady basis in our parks have been covered in some detail by firsthand accounts of rangers in our national parks. What makes a person want to be a national park ranger? Park rangers are people who care about our country's natural resources and about its people. Rangers are people who want to see those resources protected from vandalism and from destruction, while protecting park visitors as well.

Rangers have various personal reasons for becoming rangers. It is certainly not for the salary. National park rangers are notoriously underpaid. The major reasons rangers choose this line of work include: love of the outdoors, a desire to keep the national parks scenic, a love of wildlife, a desire to serve and protect the public, an interest in natural processes, and a desire to keep the parks crime free.

Rangers make frequent contacts with many visitors, including dangerous violators. All of these contacts require special tactics to meet various situations., In order to be prepared for these contacts, rangers must be carefully trained and educated in police defense tactics and in psychological tactics. The ranger must possess a keen sense of observation and awareness. The ranger must be able to interact with the violator as a friend, a guardian, a confessor, an educator, and as a professional. In other words, a ranger must have the patience of Job, the constitution of Hercules and the wisdom of Solomon.

I believe it is important for all professionals to know what they can and cannot do on the job. Larry C. Harmon put forth this list of rangers do's and don'ts.

Do:

- Listen to the public rather than talk to them. Everyone has a story to tell.

- Empathize with their problems. See things from their point of view.

- Smile and be friendly, you can win amy supporters that way.

- Inform the public about the National Park Service.

- Help the public whenever there is an opportunity. Helping change a tire, launch a boat, or build a fire are ways in which the employee can reap benefits for the National Park Service.

- Provide first aid to injured visitors. A simple application of a bandage can make a friend forever.

Don't:

- Wear sunglasses when talking to someone. People like to look into your eyes when they talk. Use eye contact.

- Smoke in public. Park rangers have an image as all-American. Smoking tends to destroy that image.

- Use your gun or gunbelt as a place to rest your hands. This tends to emphasize the fact that you are wearing a weapon.

- Sit in your patrol vehicle and talk to a visitor.

- Come on too strong with people. An easygoing friendly attitude is necessary. Don't let caution fly away, however. The goal is low-key, not no sense.

- Play with the tools of your trade. I am referring to your pepper spray, handcuffs, and your firearm. Act like a professional.

Rangers are expected to work until a job is completed, even in an emergency rescue, such as the situation related by Larry Clark, Chief Ranger of the Glen Canyon National Recreation Area.

— Real Life Situation ————————

A small boy fell through a snow bridge in Olympic National Park. He was with his parents, and they were walking along a path. He fell through to the creek below onto a big cobble rock; the boy broke his leg.

They got him out and onto the snow. One parent walked out to the trailhead and drove down to the ranger station. The rangers radioed for a helicopter. The helicopter flew up to Appleton Pass and couldn't locate the boy. There was no place for the helicopter to land so the crew had to jump out while the helicopter hovered. They threw their packs off and dropped onto the grass 15 feet below. The rangers picked up their gear and found the boy and his parents. They were on a very steep snow field. They treated the boy, placed him on a sled, and took him to an ice field where the helicopter could land to pick him up. The helicopter came in too close to a high wall while trying to pick the boy up and almost crashed into the wall. The rangers quickly moved out of the way and slipped across the ice while trying to move the boy to safety. They almost lost lives.

THE FINAL FRONTIER

To the visitor of our national parks, the parks seem like the last strongholds of wilderness. The backcountry is still a place where time seems to have stood still. This may be the way it looks to the common observer, but it is not true. The backcountry areas of our parks have been severely impacted by many factors. Factors such as logging, mining, agriculture, and livestock grazing. The parks have to be protected from encroachments of all kinds. The job is not an easy one. Occasionally you will have to work in an area where all the local residents "hate" you. They may all hate you because they perceive you as someone who is limiting their freedom to do exactly as they want with the parks.

The Coulee Dam National Recreation Area is a prime example of rampant hatred of the park service by local residents. The area was established in 1946 by the Secretary of the Interior's approval of the Tri-Part Agreement which included the National Park Service, the Bureau of Reclamation, and the Bureau of Indian Affairs. Under the agreement, the National Park Service would manage the area as a unit of the National Park Service. The local residents wanted to retain control of the land directly adjoining the new lake, which was created by the Grand Coulee Dam on the Columbia River. The land along the lake rightfully belongs to all the citizens of our country. The local residents insist upon encroaching upon these lands. They build docks onto the lake and maintain this lakeshore as private property. The visitor feels unable to utilize some of the best beaches on the lake because of this encroachment. The local residents have been cited and arrested for these violations. The animosity over the use of Lake Roosevelt lakeshore continues to grow. The rangers must not let themselves be affected from intense dislike, instead all people should be treated objectively and the resource should be protected emphatically.

Through the fault of careless visitors and unscientific management of our parks in past years, many problems have crept past the park's boundaries, such as exotic plants and plant diseases, burros, and devastating forest fires. Rangers are called upon in each of these instances to protect the parks. The burro removal project in the Grand Canyon was totally performed by rangers.

Law enforcement rangers participate in burro control in the Grand Canyon, elk control in the Grand Tetons, firefighting in Yellowstone and elsewhere, buffalo control in Theodore Roosevelt, and noxious weed control in all parks.

Rangers even set fires to control the buildup of fuel in many areas. Fire is a necessary tool for the propagation of some tree species, such as the giant sequoia. After the first year of controlled burning in Sequoia National Park, 6,000 sequoia seedlings sprouted.

The ranger must be conscious of the extreme feelings that many visitors have concerning fire, wildlife and even the nation's symbol against fire, Smoky the Bear.

The only good way to gain this expertise is to obtain as much training and education in natural processes as you can. There are many schools which offer courses in fire ecology and wildlife ecology. Learn why these processes are important. The visitor needs to hear the explanation from a ranger. The National Park Service ranger is important. Visitors take what a ranger tells them as "gospel." Don't let the visitor down. Do your homework before you put on the uniform and strap on the defensive equipment.

People support the idea that parks should be places where wildlife are protected. Rangers do the protecting. Rangers are even responsible for introducing species which have long been missing from the parks. Wolves have been reintroduced to Yellowstone National Park, panthers may someday return to the Everglades, and the red wolf to the South. These predators were once the "bad" animals in our parks. They preyed on deer, elk, moose, and bison. Then, it was a ranger's job to exterminate these animals. Today, it is our job as rangers to reinform visitors about the natural processes in which these predators play an important part. This important function of predators is best illustrated by what happened to Yellowstone's elk herds once the wolves and mountain lions wee eliminated from that park. The Yellowstone elk herds increased dramatically. The herd overflowed the park's boundaries and impacted rancher's hay fields and cattle pastures. The winter of 1919-1920 was so severe that the park's herd faced a massive die off from starvation. The herd was not being controlled by natural predation. It was the job of the ranger to live trap the elk from their herds. According to Everhart, 10,000 elk were live trapped in Yellowstone and shipped to 39 different

states. This effort is responsible for the comeback in elk populations and elk hunting in our western states. This effort, as successful as it was, still didn't reduce the herd to a reasonable level. It was
decided by park management to eliminate excess animals by
shooting them, this too fell on the rangers. This final tactic
worked, the herds were successfully reduced to sustainable levels.
Now, predators are allowed to naturally thin the herds. The ranger
is still responsible for the control and protection of the wildlife
within the park's boundaries. The ranger is also responsible for the
protection of the facilities in the parks.

PARK FACILITIES

Park facilities are always in need of repair and renewal.
Perhaps, the time has come to eliminate many of these amenities
from within the parks' boundaries. Too much emphasis has been
placed upon providing roads for larger and larger recreational
vehicles and other vehicles. The provision of electrical hookups
so visitors can watch their televisions while vacationing, and
sewage and water hookups for their hot showers should also go the
way of the automobile—out! It is up to the park ranger of
tomorrow to explain to the visitor why it is important to eliminate
this improper" use of our scenic parks. The national parks have
reached a crucial crossroads to their history.

Environmentalists and conservationists are becoming alarmed
by the misuse of helicopters at the Grand Canyon for sight-seeing,
the entry of cruise ships into Glacier Bay, hang gliding in Yosemite,
snowmobiling in Yellowstone and hunting in the Grand Tetons.
Free-lance environmentalists and radical groups, such as "Earth
Firsters," are calling for the elimination of automobiles from the
national parks (Scarce). Edward Abbey wrote, "No more cars in
the national parks. Let the people walk or ride horses, bicycles, or
mules, wild pigs—anything—but keep the automobiles and motorcycles and all their motorized relatives out." Abbey was an
outright individualist, he said what he wanted, when he wanted.
Rangers must see to it that all of these viewpoints are allowed to
be expressed.

   Brower, the head of the Sierra Club during the dam crisis on the Grand Canyon, published a full page advertisement in the *New York Times* and the *Washington Post* urging public opposition. Many rangers supported this position. The next day the Internal Revenue Service warned the Club that its tax exempt status was in danger. The Club ignored the warning, and placed another advertisement stating, "Should we also flood the Sistine Chapel so tourists can get nearer the ceiling?" This argument presented to the American public turned the tide in favor of preserving our natural heritage, not destroying it. In this case, Brower controlled the show. The National Park Service has been influenced by these groups in one sense or another since its inception. The difference is the amount of influence groups such as the Sierra Club can now muster. The victory in stopping the Grand Canyon dams marked a turning point in American history; the expensive, huge projects will never be taken for granted again. The era of conflict, however, is not over.

   The major innovations today are in the development of highly organized citizen's groups to serve as pressure groups in preservation causes. The citizen groups have made shrewd use of litigation to gain leverage in the decision making process of agencies such as the National Park Service. The decisions, which were once made by government bureaucrats, are now being made in conjunction with groups of concerned citizens, including rangers who sometimes are members of these various groups. Through litigation, they and major public interest law firms have created the field of environmental law (Irland).

   In Florida, the environmentalist groups turned their ire on another industry, the transportation industry. The transportation industry was crucial to the national parks in the beginning. Stephen Mather was able to enlist the support of the auto and highway lobby, as well as the railroads, in the early days of the National Park Service. Nowadays, it is air travel that is on the leading edge of the transportation industry. It is also the same industry, air transportation, that posed a threat to park preservation. In Florida's Everglades National Park, preservation groups have again beat back an effort to replace park wilderness with runways (Alin). Dade County, Florida wanted to built a large jetport. The supporters of this project were local residents, the airlines, and local politicians. The development of such a jetport would boost the local economy dramatically. The proposed site was on private land, six miles from Everglades National Park. State, local and federal authorities were powerless to prevent the development. Environmentalists warned that the proposed development would destroy the ecosystem of the Everglades National Park. The park depends upon the water that flows into it. The park boundaries might remain safe, but without the water, the park would die. Florida's conservation groups and the Miami chamber of commerce were responsible for the passage of a House bill that provided for the condemnation of a 570,000 acre tract immediately north of the park. This move assured the temporary safety of Everglades National Park. The success of this movement was only possible through the action of private interest groups.

The National Park Service has accepted environmental principles as well as the criticisms which have been leveled at the service from various environmental groups. "In a sense, these are pressure groups on us to keep us. . . in line, but I like to look at them as supporters, because really that's what they are. They give us a lot of flak, and we get up in arms, you know, but they are friends too."(Foresta) The park service actually considers these groups to be natural allies, much to the chagrin of would-be exploiters, says Chief Ranger Bruce Edmonston of Craters of the Moon National Monument.

Americans must be made aware of the problems facing their national parks. These problems will be shared and solved by all Americans through education and action. The educational process should include setting standards for entry into our parks and camping ethics for all users.

Automobile access into the parks may need to be reduced or even eliminated. Mass transportation must be devised and implemented. The capacity of each park must be determined. When capacity is reached, limits on visitation must be imposed. This could be accomplished by instituting a reservation system and increasing visitor fees. All concessions must be evaluated. If a concession is found to be unnecessary, then it should be removed. Removing concessions to outside park boundaries may be a consideration. Don Hummel, a former concession owner in many of our national parks, writes, "The nation's environmental groups seem devoted to what you call the 'Lock it up and keep them out' philosophy. Leading environmentalists use the catch word of 'ecological sensitivity' to protect America's scenic treasures from people who own them."

Regardless of how private enterprise feels about the National Park System, it is here to stay. Environmentalists and conservationists would all agree on one point—the national parks are worth preserving. If that means the elimination of commercial interests of all kinds, then that is what will be done. It is time for a new nature policy within the National Park System. Today's national park rangers are at the head of this vanguard. Enforcement of the rules and regulations is essential to preserving the parks. New rangers are needed to carry on the job. Are you ready for a career that is rewarding and fulfilling?

The national parks are special. Civilization has produced many technical wonders, but it has never produced a national park. Who can manufacture a geyser, Yosemite Falls, a mud pot, a glacier, or a grizzly bear? Americans must be taught to respect and enjoy our national treasures. If we misuse and destroy them, there will never be another national park. Aldo Leopold once said, "Recreational development is a job, not of building roads into lovely country, but of building receptivity into the still unlovely human mind."

From the establishment of Yellowstone National Park to Mission 66 to the present time, the rangers of the National Park Service have served the people of the world. We have saved people from death and explained the workings of a geyser. We have arrested felons wanted for murder, and we have extinguished forest fires. The ranger will continue to serve the public. Hopefully, you will be one of the proud rangers who wear the green and grey of the National Park Service.

References

Cubbage, Frederick W., Jay O'Laughlin, and Charles S. Bullock III., *Forest Resource Policy* (NY:John Wiley and Sons) 1993.

Everhart, William C., *The National Park Service* (NY: Praeger Publishers) 1972.

Foresta, Ronald A., *America's National Parks and Their Keepers* (Washington D.C.:Resources for the Future) 1984.

Frome, Michael, *Regreening the National Parks* (Tuscon: Univ. of Arizona Press) 1992.

Frome, Michael, *Conscience of a Conservationist* (Knoxville:The Univ. of Tennesseee Press) 1989.

Hampton, Duane H.,*How the U.S. Calvalry Saved Our National Parks* (Bloomington:Indiana University Press) 1971.

Harmon, Larry C. "How to Make Park Law Enforcement Work for You," *Parks and Recreation*, Dec. 1979,   pp.20-21.

Hummel, Don, *Stealing the National Parks:The Destruction of Concessions and Park Access* (Bellevue,WA:The Free Enterprise Press) 1987.

Irland, Lloyd C., *Wilderness Economics and Policy* (MA: D.C. Heath and Co.) 1979.

Paehlke, Robert C., *Environmentalism and the Future of Progressive Politics* (New Haven: Yale University Press) 1989.

Rosenbaum, Walter A., *Environmental Politics and Policy* (Washington D.C.:Congressional Quarterly Press) 1991.

Runte, Alfred, *National Parks, The American Experience* (Lincoln: University of Nebraska Press) 1979.

Runte, Alfred, *Yosemite, The Embattled Wilderness* (Lincoln:University of Nebraska Press) 1990.

Scarce, Rik, *Eco-Warriors: Understanding the Radical Environmental Movement* (Chicago:The Noble Press) 1990.

Vig, Norman J. and Michael E. Kraft, *Environmental Policy in the 1990s* (Washington D.C.: Congressional Quarterly Press) 1990.

Wirth, Conrad L., *Parks, Politics, and the People* (Norman, OK:University of Oklahoma Press) 1980.

America's Most Popular
Practical Police Books

Criminal Law $37.95
California Criminal Codes $37.95
California Criminal Procedure 3rd $37.95
California Criminal Procedure Workbook $19.95
California's Dangerous Weapons Laws $9.95
Community Relations Concepts 3rd $37.95
Courtroom Survival $16.95
Criminal Evidence 3rd $37.95
Criminal Interrogation 3rd $19.95
Criminal Procedure 2nd $37.95
Criminal Procedure (*Case approach*) 4th $44.95
Effective Training $29.95
Exploring Juvenile Justice $37.95
Encyclopedic Dictionary of Criminology $19.95
Evidence and Property Management $29.95
Florida's Criminal Justice System $14.95
Fingerprint Science 2nd $19.95
Gangs, Graffiti, and Violence $14.95
Getting Promoted $29.95
Inside American Prisons and Jails $19.95
Introduction to Corrections $44.95
Introduction to Criminal Justice 2nd $44.95
Introduction to Criminology $44.95
Investigating a Homicide Workbook $14.95
Legal Aspects of Police Supervision $24.95
Legal Aspects of Police Supervision Case Book $24.95
The New Police Report Manual $14.95
NPS Law Enforcement $19.95
Officers At Risk (*Stress Control*) $19.95
Organized Crime: A World Perspective $29.95
Paradoxes of Police Work $14.95
PC 832 Concepts IV $24.95
Police Patrol Operations $37.95
Police Report Writing Essentials $14.95
Practical Criminal Investigation 4th $37.95
Search and Seizure Handbook 5th $19.95
Traffic Investigation and Enforcement 3rd $31.95
Understanding Street Gangs $19.95
Shipping costs: $5.00 for first item and 50¢ for each additional item.

All prices are quoted in U.S. Dollars. International orders add $10.00 for shipping.

Credit card orders only, call:

1-800-223-4838

Nevada Residents add 7¼% Sales Tax.

Unconditionally Guaranteed!
Internet http://www.copperhouse.com/copperhouse